A U.S. SPY IN IRELAND

First published in 1999 by
Marino Books
an imprint of Mercier Press
16 Hume Street Dublin 2
Tel: (01) 661 5299; Fax: (01) 661 8583
E.mail: books@marino.ie

Trade enquiries to CMD Distribution
55A Spruce Avenue
Stillorgan Industrial Park
Blackrock County Dublin
Tel: (01) 294 2556; Fax: (01) 294 2564
E.mail: cmd@columba.ie

© Martin S. Quigley 1999
Foreword © T. Ryle Dwyer
ISBN 1 86023 095 4

10 9 8 7 6 5 4 3 2 1

A CIP record for this title is available
from the British Library

Cover design by Penhouse Design
Cover photographs courtesy of the
author

Printed in Ireland by ColourBooks,
Baldoyle Industrial Estate, Dublin 13

A U.S. Spy in Ireland

Martin S. Quigley

Foreword by T. Ryle Dwyer

Marino

for Katherine

ACKNOWLEDGEMENTS

Joseph G. E. Hopkins, teacher, editor and lifelong friend; Larry McDonald, archivist, US National Archives, who discovered my Irish OSS documents in 1997; John Taylor, military-documents expert at US National Archives; B. H. Custer, volunteer at US National Archives; Michael Glazier, Irish-born publisher and editor; Loretta Daniele, word-processor in New Rochelle, New York; John Shepardson, son of Whitney Shepardson, OSS Strategic Intelligence Chief; Robert C. Nicholas, son of R. Carter Nicholas, OSS Irish Desk Head; Geoffrey M. T. Jones, President of Veterans of OSS

Contents

Foreword by T. Ryle Dwyer   11

Part I

  1   The Spy Business   27
  2   Rocky Road to Dublin   47
  3   Hazards of the Job   61
  4   An End of Partition?   79
  5   There's a Neutrality On   97
  6   Back at OSS Headquarters   109

Part II

     Text of OSS Reports   115

Coda   206
Appendix: An Espionage Primer   208
Index   216

FOREWORD BY T. RYLE DWYER

During World War II the United States sent several intelligence agents to Ireland. These agents included the head of their whole operation, William J. Donovan, but he visited openly. A second man was sent undercover to travel around Ireland for a few weeks just after America entered the war. As a result of his report three undercover agents were selected and stationed in Ireland.

Two of these agents were promptly uncovered by the Irish, who welcomed them because the Dublin government felt it had nothing to hide from the Americans. A liaison was established between Irish military intelligence and the Americans. Later, other American intelligence officers visited Ireland for discussions and, at the request of the Irish government, another agent was stationed in the country until the end of the war. Only one American intelligence officer, Martin S. Quigley, retained his cover in Ireland throughout his wartime stay.

His story does not have the cloak-and-dagger-type excitement of a spy movie; it is instead the story of the mundane transmission of information. Many misconceptions about Irish neutrality had developed abroad during the war, and Quigley's mission was to find out what was really happening in Ireland. He was, in effect, double-checking on what the uncovered agents had been either shown or allowed to observe.

There had been rumours of German parachutists and Japanese tourists roaming the country and of U-boat bases dotted around the Irish coast, and fanciful stories had been published about their crews drinking in Irish pubs. Quigley's story would no doubt have been much more exciting had the various rumours been true, but they were not. His account is of what he actually found in Ireland.

Spies sent abroad are normally told only what they need to know, with the result that Quigley knew very little about what the other agents were doing. Therefore in order to put the Quigley mission in context it is necessary to give a brief history of American intelligence operations in Ireland during World War II.

Prior to America's entry into the war following the attack on Pearl Harbour, William J. Donovan was selected by President Franklin D. Roosevelt to establish the Co-ordination of Information Bureau, the country's first central intelligence agency. Donovan visited Dublin on 8 March 1941 in an effort to persuade the Taoiseach, Éamon de Valera, to allow the Americans to build a naval base on Lough Swilly in County Donegal. The visit was made to coincide with secret Anglo-American talks being held in Washington, where it was decided that Americans would begin building a base in the north of Ireland and take charge of it once the United States became an active belligerent.

Believing that Lough Swilly was more suitable than any port in Northern Ireland, Donovan approached de Valera. The Taoiseach, however, explained that he could not risk becoming embroiled in the war by giving bases to anyone. As a result, the base was subsequently built on nearby Lough Foyle in Northern Ireland.

Secretary of State Cordell Hull was possibly unaware of the nature of the Donovan mission a few weeks later when he publicly denied that the US had ever asked for the Irish base. 'Lough Swilly,' Hull said, 'would be scarcely any improvement over Lough Foyle, twenty miles away over the border in Northern Ireland and already being used by the British'.

Following the attack on Pearl Harbour and Germany's declaration of war on the United States in December 1941, Donovan sent a spy to Ireland to make a quick evaluation of what was going on in the country. Robert D. Patterson, who served for a number of years as US Consul in Cork during the 1930s, was chosen for the mission. He set out with 'a considerable supply of silk stockings, lipsticks, sugar, coffee, lemons and tea'.

Patterson planned to spend three weeks moving around the twenty-six counties of Éire. His cover was trying to interest the editors of local newspapers in publishing excerpts from a regular bulletin being sent out by the US Embassy in London. While travelling about he distributed his supplies in order to get people to talk more freely. He reported that almost everyone he talked with brought up the thorny question of the ports that de Valera had denied to the British.

'You're here for no good,' the manageress of a Cahir hotel said to Patterson. 'I suppose it's the forts and ports you want.'

While in Kerry he was alarmed to learn that there had supposedly been a lot of German activity, especially in the Tralee area, which he described as 'the hot spot'. He reported that 'several German parachutists had been picked up both going to Dublin and on their way to Killarney'. Just why he thought they were going to Killarney, one can only wonder.

Did he believe they wished to see the famed lakes? He was probably the victim of some Kerryman's sense of humour.

Three German warplanes had crash-landed in different parts of Kerry but all twenty-five airmen were quickly arrested and interned at the Curragh. A German spy had also been landed from a U-boat near Dingle. He buried his radio, which was quickly found, and was arrested by detectives from Tralee within a matter of hours as he tried to make his way to Dublin on a train.

Patterson had some personal contacts in Kerry, including Harry O'Meara, the Garda Chief Superintendent in Tralee, who told him that someone from the German Legation made a trip to the vicinity practically every week and visited 'homes all round Tralee'. O'Meara reportedly added that 'one small German radio receiving and sending set' had been picked up 'about a year ago' and that another was 'known to exist but had not been located.'

'I don't know what the hell you're doing here,' O'Meara said, 'but you're welcome.'

Patterson's alarmist report fitted neatly into a critical picture of Irish neutrality that was already being formed in Washington. For instance, American intelligence had been particularly suspicious of Secretary of the Department of External Affairs Joseph P. Walshe. Donovan informed President Roosevelt that he had learned from an 'entirely reliable source' that in April 1941 Walshe had advised the German Minister in Dublin that the Axis powers should not postpone their invasion of Britain beyond the following spring because America would probably be in the war by then.

That summer, when the Coordination of Information Bureau gave way to the Office of Strategic Services, the wartime forerunner of the CIA, the Americans were further disturbed by reports that Walshe and the German Minister spent their summer holiday near one another in County Kerry, and David Gray, the US Minister to Ireland, passed on to President Roosevelt a warning from a rather bizarre source, the supposed ghost of former British Prime Minister A. J. Balfour. On 15 February 1942 Gray sent the president the transcript of the seance at the minister's residence in Phoenix Park, where Balfour's ghost supposedly warned that Walshe was 'hand in glove' with the Germans.

Gray was in a position to cause alarm in the highest circles in the United States because he had direct access to the White House. His wife, Maud, was an aunt of Eleanor Roosevelt, the president's wife. The relationship was particularly close as Maud was only six years Eleanor's senior and Maud's mother reared Eleanor as well Maud. As a result the two women were more like sisters.

In his covering letter to the president, Gray noted that W. T. Cosgrave, the leader of the Irish opposition, had privately told him of having secret information suggesting that Walshe might be scheming against the Dublin government.

It was hardly surprising, in the circumstances, that the Americans decided to station some agents in Ireland. The film star Errol Flynn, whose father had been a professor at Queen's University, Belfast, was one of the first to volunteer. Donovan suggested to Roosevelt that Flynn should be sent openly in uniform to drum up Irish support for the American war effort, but Patterson warned that such a move would be pointless because the Irish were so scared of becoming involved in the war that it would 'do no good to ask them for anything or to send high-powered salesmen'.

The OSS selected three men to go to Ireland as undercover agents. One was Ervin Ross 'Spike' Marlin, who had studied at Trinity College, Dublin, from 1929 to 1932 after securing a degree in Celtic Studies from Columbia University, New York. He was attached to the American Legation as a special assistant to Gray, advising on economic matters and was given the code name 'Hurst'.

Marlin took up his post in Dublin on 4 September 1942 but his cover was blown almost immediately when material was forwarded to him in the ordinary mail with a covering letter to the effect that the material had been requested by the OSS. The letter was opened by the Irish censor, so Marlin knew that Irish officials were aware that he was an intelligence agent, but no effort was made to have him recalled. He was welcomed as an independent witness who would, it was hoped, correct the distorted picture of Irish policy being painted by the irascible Gray.

Initially Marlin confined himself to Dublin. Towards the end of November 1942 he travelled to London to make his first full report on his findings in Ireland. 'There is undoubtedly Axis activity in Éire,' he wrote. 'Just how much there is I do not know because I have only been in Dublin, and the Axis works almost exclusively outside Dublin.'

The second OSS agent, Roland Blenner-Hassett, had taken up his position in Tralee in late September 1942. He was to find out what was really happening in that supposed 'hot spot' of Nazi activity. He had been born and reared in the town but emigrated to the United States during the struggle for independence in the 1920s and had secured a doctorate in philology from Harvard University. His cover was that he was collecting folklore material. Initially he was meant to report to Marlin, but the two men could not get on.

Marlin, who thought that Blenner-Hassett was a British academic because of his cultivated accent, described him to me as 'a frightful snob'. Blenner-Hassett was actually from quite humble origins. His real name was Roland Hassett: he had added the 'Blenner-' prefix to his surname in the United States. Many of the local people considered him a social climber who was ashamed of his origins. They thought he was trying to pass himself off as a member of the Blennerhassett family, which owned Ballyseedy Castle and formed part of the old Protestant gentry in the Tralee area. The fact that he also tended to be outspokenly critical of the Catholic Church, of which he had once been a member, did little to endear him to the stridently Catholic community.

Blenner-Hassett was quickly uncovered by the Irish as an OSS agent but, as with Marlin, no effort was made to expel or arrest him. Instead the authorities agreed to allow him to have the same diplomatic privileges that Marlin's official position afforded him for reporting. No doubt they hoped that he, too, would correct Gray's distorted reports. Marlin was even assisted in his investigations of the rest of the country with a monthly ration of petrol, which was restricted to essential services at the time.

Martin's first trip outside Dublin was to the west coast, where he had a long discussion with one of the heroes of the War of Independence, Ernie O'Malley, who dismissed as nonsense all talk of significant collusion between the IRA and Germany. Elsewhere the story was essentially the same.

Marlin therefore concluded that his initial report about

German activities outside Dublin was unfounded. Indeed, he came to realise that most of the stories about German spies were ludicrous. 'The whole thing was a kind of joke,' he later recalled. 'I spoke to J. P. Walshe, who told me that there were between fifty and a hundred thousand British sympathisers in Éire who were straining at the leash to report anything they heard about German spies.' Marlin never personally uncovered any spies, nor did he find any indication of the existence of spy centres. 'I assumed that Irish intelligence had the place buttoned up,' he explained. 'Once they realised it was in their interest to keep us informed, they were very good to us.'

On 4 January 1943 Marlin informed OSS headquarters that both Gray and himself had been approached separately by Walshe with an offer to arrange cooperation with the United States on intelligence matters. Gray, whose distrust of de Valera bordered on paranoia, opposed Marlin's involvement for fear the Irish would somehow seek to use this to embarrass the American Legation.

In mid-January, Blenner-Hassett was called over to London to make a full report on his findings during his four months in Ireland. He firmly scotched speculation about Nazi intrigue in Kerry and corroborated Marlin's conclusion. Of course, in both of their cases the Irish had been aware they were OSS agents throughout the bulk of their period in Ireland. As a result, the Americans were still anxious to get a strictly undercover agent into Ireland.

In order not to compromise his cover, great care was taken that no strings were seen to be pulled to facilitate Quigley's mission to Ireland. As he mentions in this book, he was given a code password by which he could identify himself to

Marlin if he needed help, but he never used this. By then relations between Gray and Marlin had become so strained that the OSS officer found it easier to work out of the American Embassy in London, from where he continued to liaise with the Irish on intelligence matters.

Quigley's role was to report what he saw rather than go digging for secret information. His reports were written in such a way as not to rouse any suspicion about him should anybody get hold of them. He confirmed what Marlin and Blenner-Hassett had found before him. Unlike those two men, Quigley was a down-to-earth person who probably had more in common with Marlin but had an added touch of diplomatic finesse that enabled him to keep his opinions to himself. Marlin was a forceful character who was not afraid to express his opinions, which probably explains many of his problems with Gray, a similar character. Had their opinions coincided there would probably have been no problems, but they tended to see the Irish authorities from very different perspectives. Gray came from the hunting, fishing and shooting set and was much more at home with the old landed gentry, who tended to think of themselves as more Anglo than Irish, while Marlin was more a man of the people. On the other hand, Blenner-Hassett was, in the minds of his contemporaries, 'a frightful snob' who was trying pass himself off as being from the landed class.

In this book Quigley makes it clear that 'the use of the term "neutral" as applied to the twenty-six counties of Éire was a misnomer': he notes that the Dublin government provided a great deal of secret help to the Allies, whereas it never gave any help to Germany. He explains, for instance, that 'communications of Éire diplomats stationed abroad were made available to the US government'.

The American military was actually quite happy with de Valera's policy. The Irish had been handing over so much good intelligence information that Marlin was ordered to sound out Dublin in July 1943 about the possibility of securing Irish help for espionage activities on the Continent by having Irish diplomats transmit information. Marlin reported that Walshe responded favourably after consulting de Valera.

Since this opened the possibility of using Irish diplomats as American spies, it was decided that R. Carter Nicholas, the head of the Éire Desk at the strategic-intelligence division of the OSS, should visit Dublin. On 25 September 1943 he and Marlin conferred with Walshe.

'I told Walshe that the information which had been received as a result of the liaison had been very useful,' Nicholas reported. 'I then said that the rapid progress of the war was fixing attention more and more on information from the Continent and I wished to sound out the possibility of Irish help, including in particular the possibility of our receiving information from Irish diplomatic sources.'

De Valera authorised a system whereby Marlin would supply the Department of External Affairs with questions for Irish representatives in Berlin, Rome, the Vatican and Vichy. Walshe would then forward their replies to Marlin. Whether the Irish diplomats realised it or not, they were being used as American spies.

Gray remained unhappy, however. He began to look to the postwar period and concluded that there was a danger that de Valera would create difficulties between Britain and America by appealing to Irish-Americans to use their political muscle to put pressure on the White House to force the British to end the partition of Ireland. In order to undermine de Valera's standing, Gray suggested that Roosevelt should ask for the use of Irish bases in such a way as to provoke the Taoiseach's refusal. In that way he could depict the Taoiseach as unhelpful to the Allies.

The American Joint Chiefs of Staff were unwilling to take any chance that de Valera would agree to hand over the bases because they did not want to run the risk of Ireland coming into the war. They advised that Roosevelt should ask the Irish government to promise to make bases available only in the event of the United States needing them, but Churchill killed that idea because he was afraid that de Valera would comply and would thus be in a better position than ever to raise the partition issue. At this point Quigley was withdrawn from Ireland and sent to Italy.

Quigley was the only American agent sent to Ireland who remained undercover throughout his stay. There is no doubt that Dan Bryan was suspicious of his presence and would undoubtedly have had people keeping an eye on him, but Quigley successfully reported on his work.

While in Ireland, Quigley travelled extensively and met a wide range of people, including de Valera, Frank Aiken, W. T. Cosgrave, Richard Mulcahy, Sean T. O'Kelly, Gerald Boland, various newspaper editors and a number of bishops, including Archbishop John Charles McQuaid.

Like most Americans who visited Ireland during the war, Quigley thought it would be possible to arrange a deal whereby the Allies could use Irish bases in return for the ending of Partition, the causes of which he analysed in some depth. Churchill secretly offered Dublin such a deal in June

1940 but de Valera rejected it.

Quigley's choice of Emmet Dalton as a conduit to sound out the British was particularly apt because Dalton had been a military adviser to Michael Collins during the Treaty negotiations of 1921 and had participated in the Treaty negotiations between Collins and Churchill on defensive matters. As a result, he probably had access to Downing Street.

Quigley mentions many meetings with the film censor, Dr Richard Hayes, who was coincidentally working very closely with Irish military intelligence due to the fact that he was a brilliant code-breaker. In fact, he broke a number of the codes being used by German spies sent to Ireland. In order to preserve his cover, Quigley concentrated in his reports on matters relating to films.

Quigley provides some rare insights into the thinking of the time. For instance, Hayes told him that he was 'very much against South American- and South Seas-type dancing' on moral grounds and consequently sought to ban such films. De Valera told Quigley that he believed film had great educational potential. Of course, this meant it was also a means of propaganda, which probably explains why de Valera was prepared to go along with the wide-ranging cuts made by the censor.

The form of propaganda may sometimes have been subtle, but usually it was blatant, and the fact that the government did not want any debate on the neutrality issue meant that there was extensive censorship. Even the sentiments of prominent members of the Catholic Church were censored. Quigley was particularly surprised when the censor banned 'The Eternal Gift,' a purely religious film produced by the

Servite Fathers with a foreword by the Archbishop of Chicago and commentary by Monsignor Fulton J. Sheen. De Valera explained, however, that 'this country is so Catholic that representation of a Catholic religious service, no matter how treated, would be objectionable.'

During the Civil War de Valera had defied the bishops, and he might have feared that Quigley would therefore suspect his Catholic credentials, so in his own subtle way he let Quigley know that his half-brother, Father Thomas Wheelwright, was a priest. 'At the door of his office de Valera asked whether I had met his brother, a priest in the United States,' Quigley reported.

Of course, censorship was not related solely to the personal views of a few people such as the censor, de Valera and Frank Aiken, the minister in charge of censorship. Others, like the Catholic Archbishop of Dublin, John Charles McQuaid, had a major influence. McQuaid apparently had a French film on the Passion banned. The Papal Nuncio, Pascal Robinson, told Quigley that he would not care to see such a film himself but would not object to others seeing it. He was of course overruled in Dublin, however, by McQuaid, who was almost a law unto himself, even in the early days of his reign.

'Other bishops resented the fact that his influence with the Film Censor achieves control of films in their dioceses,' Quigley noted. 'One is frequently told the story in Ireland about there being not "twenty-six bishops there but twenty-six popes".' The Bishop of Limerick, for instance, may not have had much influence with the film censor but he nonetheless had all films banned in Limerick on Sundays.

A US Spy in Ireland gives the first inside look at the life of an Allied spy in Ireland, as well as affording an honest American evaluation of the wartime reality of this country's foreign policy, which was deliberately distorted by the Roosevelt administration for its own political purposes. Although Quigley's wartime reports cover little more than a six-month period, they provide an example of how intelligence information can be transmitted in innocuous business reports and offer some fascinating insights into the Ireland of 1943.

PART I

1

THE SPY BUSINESS

It all began in Washington, DC, on a sunny November afternoon in 1942 at an apartment in a new building on Que Street NW just over the Rock Creek Bridge on the way to Georgetown. When I rang the doorbell, it was obvious that I was expected as the door was opened immediately. I found three men within, one wearing the uniform of a US Army captain.

I was there in response to a message from the head-quarters of the Strategic Intelligence Division of the Office of Strategic Services (OSS) of the United States Joint Chiefs of Staff, but it had told me no more than the address and apartment number.

The purpose of the clandestine meeting, as I was informed, was to administer the oath of office which would make me a secret intelligence officer. It was stressed that everything in connection with my OSS activities was to be forever secret. That was essential for the protection of the government and for my own security when in the United States and most especially when overseas.

The 'forever secret' mandate lasted three decades – long enough, it was thought, to protect me and my sources. I would have been content to have full secrecy last indefinitely, but the security was broken by the US government, which, over a number of years, beginning in the 1970s, gradually declassified documents which revealed my identity as an OSS agent and something of what I did. Documents concerning my work in Rome and at the Vatican in late 1944 and 1945 became available at the US National Archives in the 1980s. In 1997 – after more than half a century – further documents which dealt with my work in 1943 in neutral Ireland were declassified and made available to scholars at the new National Archives Building in College Park, Maryland.

While I took the oath of an intelligence officer with full commitment and no reservations, the role I was embarking upon in the war effort certainly was not my first choice. Like most young American men of my age, education, and beliefs, I would have preferred an active role in some branch of the US military. To most of us the best way to play our small part in helping to win the war was to be in direct contact with the enemy. That route was not open to me, however, either as a volunteer or in the draft, on account of almost crippling nearsightedness. My vision was normal when I wore glasses, but without them I could not see at three feet what should be seen at twenty.

By this time most of my friends and classmates were in military service. My closest friends were in the Navy: one was communications officer on a destroyer escort in the Atlantic battle against U-boats; another was involved with anti-submarine nets used to protect harbors; and the third, who had gone to the United States Naval Academy, was to have his ship fall victim to a Japanese kamikaze attack. Another was 'missing in action' when his US submarine was sunk in the depths of the eastern Pacific. I had already attended the wake of one college friend, an expert rifleman who had taught me the little I knew of marksmanship. He had been a member of the National Guard and Reserve Officers Training Corps and a champion marksman. In the confusion of assignments in the early months after Pearl Harbour, he was an observer in an Army Air Corps plane that crashed on anti-submarine patrol off the coast of Maryland, where a great many Allied ships were being sunk by German submarines.

Almost everyone had mixed emotions in volunteering for espionage. I know I did. Spying has had a poor public image all through history. Men and women involved in it have worked in secret and what they did or did not accomplish was usually never revealed. Inevitably espionage involves deception. Spying does not make gentlemen or ladies. Some kind of role-playing is involved in it and that does not come easy for most people.

Despite the low esteem in which many hold the intelligence profession, spies may obtain some information of great importance that can be got in no other way. Unlike several of the major powers, the United States never had a peace-time foreign secret intelligence agency until two years after the end of World War II.

As a youth I never had any particular interest in espionage. In history classes all of us had heard about such persons as Benedict Arnold. Spies and traitors were rather bunched together as not very wholesome characters.

When I was in Loyola School, a small Jesuit high school at Eighty-third Street and Park Avenue in New York City, I had an opportunity to listen for several hours to an authentic spy of World War I tell stories. On the day I took my oath of office on joining the secret intelligence division of the Office of the Strategic Services, I did not think of Fritz Hubert Duquesne – known in the early 1930s as Major Craven – but he may have been in my subconscious.

We had a family custom where at dinner our father would recount the highlights of his day at his publishing office. Since his publications were in the motion-picture field, often his reports were interesting to me and my younger sisters. One evening in the summer of 1933 he could hardly wait for the food to be on the table before he told us what had happened. On his return from lunch his general manager rushed into his office shouting, 'The police have Craven in my office and are beating him up!' Someone of the family interrupted to ask who the man was. His name, we were told, was Major Craven. He was an Englishman who had recently been hired as an advertising salesman.

My father expected something like petty larceny or writing bad checques when he asked the business manager, 'What is the charge?' But the answer was, 'Murder on the high seas.' That got father's attention considerably more than hearing an employee was being beaten up in the office by policemen.

A call to the higher-ups in the police department put an end to the violence. It then appeared that the charge of 'murder on the high seas' had been placed during World War I at the request of the British government. When the New York police got in touch with British authorities, they were told there was no interest in prosecuting fifteen years after the end of hostilities.

It turned out that Major Craven, alleged British advertising-space salesman, was actually an Afrikander, Fritz Hubert Duquesne. He, his father and other members of his family suffered in the Boer War in South Africa, and he had developed a life-long hatred of the British. His first opportunities for revenge came when he became an espionage agent of the Germans, operating for much of World War I in various countries in Latin America. At the time of his arrest in the Quigley Publishing Company office, an unauthorised biography of him had just been published under the title *The Man Who Killed Kitchener*.

According to the story – which may be true, partially true, or wholly a fable – the Boer agent had made his way from Latin America to Russia. There, posing as a Russian naval lieutenant, he made himself a part of the Russian group escorting Lord Kitchener by sea to Russia. From aboard the ship he claimed to have signalled a German submarine which sank the British warship, with the loss of Kitchener and hundreds of others. How the German submarine under such circumstances managed to pick up Fritz Duquesne is a mystery.

In the weeks after Duquesne was released my father took an interest in learning about the man's history. Duquesne was a wonderful storyteller. To check his authenticity my father had him meet with a number of persons, of whom the most prominent was Reverend Wilfrid Parsons SJ, editor of the Jesuit weekly magazine, *America*. Father Parsons's conclusion was that Duquesne did not follow a strict chronology in telling the story of his life and probably mixed some of his activities with those of his father. Yet everything that could be checked was correct. There was no doubt that the Boer agent had a great command of languages, was a

31

skilled impersonator and was widely travelled.

On one occasion I listened while Duquesne talked for several hours about the methods he used to blow up ships. His effectiveness in this work was what had caused him to be charged by the British with 'murder on the high seas.' This made a great impression on me because I had been interested in sailing since I was a young child and had recently gone to Europe on the *Statendam* of the Holland American line and returned on the *White Star*, the old *Cunard Olympic*. One of my hobbies was celestial navigation.

'Espionage' was the title I put on an article for the *Loyola*, my high school magazine. I did not name Duquesne but referred to him as 'the Master Spy' and described in some detail three methods he claimed to have used to blow up ships at sea.

An introductory paragraph of my article read, 'Spies, by the very nature of their work, earn for themselves a strange position in the eyes of men. They are admired for their indomitable courage in working alone in a strange country without tools, materials, or friends. They labour right in the heart of the enemy country, and one slight slip means death before the firing squad. The work of a spy is nevertheless fascinating. The fact that in no war has there been a lack of volunteers for this most dangerous business proves the allure of espionage. Some men like to labour alone for their country without help and without a chance of living, if discovered.'

The article ended in these words: 'Espionage always was and always will be one of the most effective weapons of war, calling for the bravest men, the shrewdest of schemers. The work of the spy calls either for admiration or disgust – depending on the point of view.'

That article, written nine years before, was completely

forgotten long before I had decided to volunteer for secret undercover work – or espionage, if you will. I certainly did not consider myself either brave or shrewd. If I should fail in a neutral country, the consequences would have been unpleasant, but there was no prospect of death by firing squad.

After the swearing-in at the Que Street apartment, my first orders were to take a particular train from Washington on a specified day and get off at the Baltimore station, the first on the express train's route north. Then I was to walk over the bridge to the other side of the tracks and descend the stairs, where I would see a car waiting to pick me up.

As I was walking across the station bridge, I was surprised by a call from a person several paces behind, 'Hello, Martin.' I stopped, turned around and responded, 'Hello, Bill.' Both of us knew instantly that we were on the same assignment. What made it a surprise was that when we had seen each other a few days earlier in an office in New York City, each of us took at face value the non-governmental foreign work each of us said he had accepted. Bill had said that he was going to Spain to represent Twentieth Century-Fox newsreels. I had said that I was going to Ireland to represent the Motion Picture Producers & Distributors of America on film censorship. Now it was obvious that we were both new OSS intelligence agents. We quickly agreed that we should not let anyone know that we knew each other's identity.

An ordinary sedan with no indication of governmental service was waiting. Our small suitcases were put in the trunk and we were driven through the suburban Baltimore countryside for about twenty minutes. The car then turned into a driveway that led to a large house, probably rented from a gentleman farmer. We were greeted there by the director, whose full name we were not told. Only first names were to be used, he said. Some members of our group had already arrived, and we met them. Bill and I were assigned to the same room on the second floor.

That evening, at an orientation session held in the dining room after the meal, we found that we numbered twelve men and were the first OSS group to live in this house, which was designated E-3. Our classes in firearms were held in E-1, another house a short drive away, where a firing range had been set up in the basement. We never saw the occupants of E-1 but assumed they also were from the OSS. There was also in the neighborhood an E-2 installation but we did not visit it.

We were reminded that we should be careful at all times not to reveal our identity or our role in the OSS to our classmates. As an exercise, however, we should try to find out what we could of the others. So far as I know, none of the group learned anything significant about Bill or me. There were clues to some. Two had arrived together in civilian clothes but wearing new military boots. Before long the rest of us discovered that they were from California and were newly commissioned Marines. One was the brother of a famous film producer. Another in the class during the three-week session let it be known that he was a DuPont. One was summoned to Washington before the training period was over because he was urgently needed at the African Desk in OSS headquarters.

The other major countries, which included Britain, France, Germany and the Soviet Union, had long-established espionage organisations whose operatives received lengthy training, but the OSS was literally starting from scratch. Owing to the American desire to get on as soon as possible with the job of winning the war, OSS strategic intelligence training was reduced to the bare essentials.

The E School's curriculum was well summarised in an official report, declassified in 1985: 'The E course included a little of everything – agent undercover techniques, intelligence gathering and reporting, an introduction to sabotage, weapons, demolitions, and the 'Fairbairn method' of self-defense, as elements of X-2 (counter-intelligence) and MO (black propaganda) work . . . There were no precedents in American pedagogical experience for the things which E was trying to do . . . It grew out of the British SOE [secret intelligence] courses at the Canadian school in 1942 and 1943, but it developed into a course which well fitted the peculiar needs of the OSS.'

Since I was to operate in neutral Ireland, much of what was taught had no direct application for me, but all of it was interesting. Instruction in the use of explosives for demolition of bridges and other strategic structures was given to our group in a large field behind the house where we were quartered. The chief instructor for this subject was an army captain, a graduate of West Point, who made no secret of his unhappiness with his assignment. He wanted to be in action with his classmates and other West Point graduates. One day he remarked: 'What shall I say to my children when they ask what I did in the war? Tell them I was in Maryland trying to teach a bunch of civilians how to handle explosives without losing a hand or worse!'

The plastic type of explosive was new at that time. We were shown how a small amount of plastic – half the size of a 12-volt dry cell – had the explosive force of a substantial amount of dynamite. In addition, the explosion of plastic could be confined to a small area, thereby increasing its force. Another advantage was that plastic could be easily disguised as, for example, a bar of soap. We were all impressed with the demonstrations, which involved the destruction of several old trees. We were less content when each of us had to fit a hunk of plastic with a detonator. If the fuse was not set right and was improperly crimped, the whole thing could blow up in your hand. Conversely, if the position of the fuse was incorrect, it would not set off the explosive. Fortunately, in our group no one was hurt.

Classes in firearms were held in the basement of the E-1 building. First of all we were told that the .45 calibre revolver, the traditional sidearm of US military officers, was virtually useless. Only experts could hit anything farther away than they could throw the weapon. The weapon of choice for many in the field was a magazine pistol that could fire twenty shots in quick succession. The rule given was, 'Always fire in bursts of two shots; never fire in the automatic position as a burst of twenty shots makes a wide pattern.'

Most of the subjects were treated classroom-style, with lectures in our house's dining room. For certain subjects experts were brought in. The drug traffic was handled by an experienced federal narcotics agent from New York who had told us that he could make a drug purchase on half an hour's notice any day in the week. Another federal agent lectured on safe-cracking. His demonstration was a source of merriment. After collecting our wallets and putting them into a safe, he was unable to open it!

Every day we spent some time learning the Morse Code for radio use. Few in the group had any previous experience of it. Those who had singing ability and an ear for music were quickest to catch on. I made very slow progress. The instructor said that if I was interested in radio work I could go to a special OSS radio school. I thanked him but said it was unlikely that I would need to do any radio transmission. In the field, trained radio operators were usually assigned to an intelligence agent or a small group of agents. In some instances, especially in work behind enemy lines, an agent was his own radio operator.

Much of what was discussed would be of use for agents destined to function in enemy countries; some of it, though, had potential value in operating under commercial cover in a neutral country. Of these, 'cover' – that is, the 'cloak' used to shield the real work of the intelligence agent – was of prime importance. Most people have some familiarity with cover through what they have read in newspapers or works of fiction. At a minimum, cover is a character that is assumed to convey a false impression but that seems genuine. For example, a thief might come to a house door carrying tools and gain admission by pretending to be a handyman or a utility-meter reader.

The espionage professional needs a deep cover – one that adequately cloaks his real work and will endure as long as he is in his operational area. The cover should also be of a character that gives the agent mobility to move about freely and travel when necessary. In many instances the cover is arranged by a superior in the intelligence organisation. Then the agent's responsibility is to become thoroughly familiar with the cover and maintain it all the time he is in the field.

The discussions of cover by the E-teaching staff had only an academic interest for me. I was one of the fortunate people who volunteered for OSS with a ready-made cover which fulfilled most of the conditions needed to make it ideal. I was to represent the trade organisation of the American motion-picture industry – and this was logical for I would have been well qualified for the position had it existed. Such a cover would give me complete freedom of movement and the ability to speak with individuals in every rank of society.

The emphasis in the curriculum on security was in some ways the most important. An intelligence organisation and everyone in it must function on a strict 'need to know' basis. Secrecy must be the byword at all times for the protection of the individual agent and his government. A breach of security – even a seemingly minor one – might make continuation of the mission impossible. A secret agent who is no longer secret cannot function. Additionally, disclosure of an agent's identity may cause serious complications at a variety of levels both inside and outside government.

An intelligence agent must be skilled in observing, interviewing, and reporting. In a three-week course there was no time to do more than stress the need for these skills. The obligation to be satisfied about qualifications in these areas had to rest on the officials at OSS headquarters who had recruited the agents and given them their assignments.

I was fortunate in having had extensive training and professional experience in reporting and writing, so I had no concerns about that part of my role as an intelligence agent. Some of the specifics taught concerning evaluation of sources seemed important, however. The same statement made by two people – one in a position to know the facts and the other with no such knowledge – might, for example, have quite different values.

A good deal of attention was given to our being followed or 'tailed'. How does one know this is happening? What actions should be taken to confirm the presence of a 'tail' without arousing suspicion? How might being tailed be useful to the agent's purpose by helping to confirm the validity of his cover?

Another interesting – and potentially useful – class dealt with steps to be taken to determine whether one's room or luggage has been searched and the need to ensure that a search could reveal nothing that would arouse suspicion of the agent's cover. One's room and luggage should always be left in a condition that would further support the cover occupation.

On Friday afternoons during the first two weeks of the E-course, the members of our group went on field assignments. The first of these provided training in a basic technique used from time immemorial, whereby two persons previously unknown to each other could verify their identities before transmitting something – a spoken or written communication or a material object of some kind. The easiest method for establishing *bona fides* was for one of the two parties to ask a short question, which the other answered in a previously set formula.

A staff instructor informed each of our group what reply he should make to a stranger who approached and asked a particular question. The man who had properly identified himself by asking the correct question would then pass something in a secret way. Our conduct during the contact would be observed by an OSS person unknown to us.

I was dropped off near a tavern or bar in downtown Baltimore and told that the pass would be made inside at an unspecified time later in the afternoon. The site was not a particularly good one for me as I was not a regular patron of bars. In fact, I was unfamiliar with 'hard' liquor and drank beer rarely. Another problem was that the bar catered to middle-aged or older local Baltimoreans – men and a few women who worked or lived in the immediate area.

I entered the bar, walked slowly across the room and sat down on one of the bar stools – choosing one that let me keep an eye on the front door. I assumed – correctly, as it turned out to – that my contact would not have arrived at the place before I did. Ordering a glass of the local beer, I drank it very slowly, giving the impression that I was waiting for a friend who was late. I passed more time looking around the room, examining the few unremarkable pictures over the bar and on the other walls. I was into my second glass of beer by this time, for I felt I couldn't twirl an empty one for long without attracting attention.

After the better part of an hour, a middle-aged man appeared who seemed to me not the type of the regular patrons but a stranger. He stood by the door for a while, looking all around at people sitting at tables, and then turned his attention to those at the dozen or so stools in front of the bar. At last he walked over to me and asked the prearranged identification question, to which I gave the set response. Only then did he take a small package from his pocket and surreptitiously slip it into my hand. I put the package in my own pocket, hoping the transaction hadn't been noticed, and we engaged in a few minutes of idle conversation, with me still sitting at the bar and the man standing next to me. He soon left, after glancing at his wristwatch, as if he remembered he had another appointment. Since we had the weekend free, I waited only a little while before leaving for a train to New York. Back at E-3 on Sunday evening, I turned in the packet to one of the staff. I never knew what was inside, as our orders did not tell us to verify what we received from our contacts.

My second field assignment was much more complex. Again we were dropped off individually at various places in the centre of the city. Each of us had the same assignment, which we were to do independent of the others in our group – get a job in a war plant without revealing one's identity. If complications arose, we were given an emergency phone number, but under no circumstances should the OSS be mentioned. Applicants for positions in war factories were supposed to have proper identification, yet our real names had to be kept secret.

I took a street car to an outlying area of the city where I knew there were several large factories making war materials. I got off near the largest of these, a Western Electric installation with buildings scattered over a large site. I soon found that hiring was handled separately by each of the several divisions. I was directed to the building of the electronics division.

On the ride out from the centre of Baltimore I had developed a strategy to avoid any questions which required documentation of my identity. The best course for me, I felt, was to tell a dazzling but plausible life story that would take the interviewer's mind off his duty to establish my identity in proper fashion. The story which I invented was that I was a screenwriter who had just flown from Hollywood to Washington. I had expected to receive a commission in the navy but had been summarily rejected. Crushed by this,

I wanted to get out of Washington as quickly as possible, so I took the first New York-bound train. During the hour from Washington to Baltimore I had decided that, barred from military service and certainly not wanting to continue writing screenplays in Hollywood comfort at such a time as the present, I would 'do my bit for the war effort' by working at a plant which made equipment to be used by fighting men. Thus, indirectly, I would play a small part in the defeat of the Nazi and Japanese war machines.

After a short wait in an outer office, I was directed to an engineer of about forty to forty-five years of age who was in charge of one of the instrument manufacturing divisions. The man was pleasant but obviously harried, short-handed and quite desperate for reasonably intelligent workers. I told my story which clearly was an unusual one. His interest quickened when I spoke of Hollywood and something of life there. In the pre-television era almost everyone was fascinated with the movies, and this engineer was no exception. He asked what shift I would work. When I said that any of the three shifts or a rotating one would be fine he could hardly restrain his delight. He was even more pleased when I said I could start on Monday morning. Then I was given a tour of the instrument assembly line and was told I would be trained to be an inspector. We shook hands and I said that I was looking forward to reporting on Monday. Anything about identity papers was overlooked, as I had hoped.

That Sunday evening I sent the engineer a Western Union night wire expressing my great regret that I was unable to report for work on Monday as I had to return to Hollywood, but I thanked him for interviewing me and offering me a position.

Back at the OSS's E-Station on Monday morning, a brief staff review was made of what each of our group had experienced. No one had had to call for emergency assistance. A number had made valiant efforts but were unsuccessful. The most ingenious report was by one of us who had made telephone calls until he found a family that had a son about his own age and learned the date of that man's birth. Going to the Baltimore city records office, he secured a copy of the young man's birth certificate. With an authentic birth certificate he had no difficulty in obtaining a position in a war plant.

At the end of the third week of classes an informal graduation party was given for our group. We sat around the dinner table discussing what we had found out about one another. I had been conscientious – as were most of the others – and at the end of the period no one, except Bill, knew any more about me than the name 'Martin.' I was the youngest by quite a few years. One of my classmates remarked, 'Martin is not being trained for this war. He is being trained for World War III.'

I certainly did not agree with that view. Nor, fortunately for me, did my OSS superiors, right up to General Donovan. Espionage is not age-related; it is related to an individual's qualifications and aptitude for a particular mission. In any event, I was not all that young. My twenty-fifth birthday occurred while I was at the E School, a fact that I of course did not reveal. By that age, men in more active services were captains of merchant ships, commanders of naval ships, squadron leaders and company commanders.

Following basic training at the E-area, I was ordered to Area RTU-11, known as 'the Farm', located somewhere in northern Virginia. The house was a very large one, accommodating about twenty people, mostly men and a few women, from various divisions of the OSS. There was no unified curriculum. Some of us were there for two weeks to learn a code system and choose personal codes. Others were there awaiting travel orders for their field stations. The accommodations were satisfactory and the food more than adequate. The staff – as at E – was friendly and cooperative. The Virginia countryside in the late fall was still beautiful, although the crops in neighbouring farms had been harvested.

During the two weeks at the Farm those of us who were to do code work had classes in the mornings and sometimes in the afternoon. In the evenings there were lectures on a variety of subjects. In free time – when we were not studying or practicing code matters – we were urged to read some of the material in the library or scattered on tables around the large living room. Most of the written material was of British origin. A particular stress was on aircraft identification – of Allied as well as enemy planes. This was of great importance to agents who were to be dropped by parachute.

Bill was not at the Farm during the time I was there, nor were any of the others who had been with me at E. So I never learned even the first name of anyone except the instructors and my roommate, a blond young man from the Midwest who was to be dropped by parachute into a country in occupied Europe. I assumed it was to be Holland. My respect and admiration for his courage and that of all the others who had similar roles in the OSS were boundless. The problems faced by agents going into neutral countries were relatively insignificant when compared with those of agents operating alone or in a small group within enemy-held territory.

At one of the first classes our instructor told us that each of us had to select two code names, one a normal English word and the other made up of five random letters. These two codes names would be kept secret from everyone except our immediate OSS superiors. Names selected should be ones that would never be forgotten. I chose for myself two variations of 'Islandhearth', the name of our home at Greenwich Cove in Riverside, Connecticut: Harte and NALSI.

OSS intelligence agents who were not likely to have access to a sophisticated cipher or code system – and were operating in areas where no coding materials, such as message pads, could be carried – were taught 'double transposition.' This was an elaboration of the simple 'Playfair' single transposition used by the British in the early days of their occupation of India.

In Playfair, we were told, each British agent was assigned a single code word. Short messages were written horizontally in boxes drawn under the code word. The letters were then lifted in vertical columns in the alphabetical order of the letters of the code word. Finally they were written in five-letter groups for dispatch to headquarters.

The Playfair code system could be broken quite quickly. If one of the OSS's 'double transposition' messages was intercepted by the enemy, it could not be decoded in less than a week, we were told.

In an emergency I was to use double transposition, assuming that I had access to radio transmission facilities. Radio access was unlikely unless there was a German invasion of neutral Ireland and an Allied military response bringing on the scene communication personnel from the OSS or other Allied military forces. Given that this was December 1942 – when the Nazi war machine still dominated Europe and threatened to invade Britain – the precaution that every OSS agent should be prepared for any emergency was clearly warranted.

For my own personal double transposition code, two different lines of poems could be used as required. The first poem I selected was a well-known one by William Blake which begins:

Tiger, Tiger, burning bright
In the forests of the night.
What immortal hand or eye
Could frame thy fearful symmetry?

Now all I had to do was wait until a way could be found to get me to Dublin with my commercial cover intact.

2

ROCKY ROAD TO DUBLIN

With an excellent commercial cover already arranged and the necessary intelligence courses completed, Francis P. Miller, a distinguished Virginian and head of the section of the OSS which included the British Empire, Afghanistan, and Ireland, expressed the hope that his new Irish agent would be in Dublin before Christmas 1942.

Then began a winter of discontent, delays, postponements, mistakes and frustrations. In addition, the security division of the organisation itself made such a blunder that the end of the mission was threatened before it even began.

There are many problems involved in getting an intelligence officer under deep commercial cover into his overseas field of activity in wartime. I ran into every conceivable one – and a couple that were so bizarre they could not be imagined in advance.

It would be difficult to imagine a more satisfactory commercial cover than that provided for me by Will H. Hays, then president of the Motion Picture Producers & Distributors of America. Hays, a Republican who had been US Postmaster General in President Warren G. Harding's cabinet, had been called to lead the American film industry in the aftermath of Hollywood scandals attributed to Fatty Arbuckle and others.

When asked to provide my cover for OSS intelligence work in Ireland, Hays immediately consented. His letter of instructions established a sound business justification for my appointment:

> Although the foreign market for American motion pictures has been seriously curtailed because of war conditions, Éire still remains open to us and that market gains additional importance from the fact that thirty-one foreign territories in which we formerly did business are now closed to us.

After recognizing that a sovereign state has the right to protect its interest through film censorship, Hays protested additional censor authority under the Emergency War Powers:

> . . . this additional authority conferred upon the official censor has caused great troubles and serious loss to the member companies of this association in recent months. Many important features have been rejected altogether and many others so mutilated as to ruin their box-office value.

Hays expressed the hope that the prolonged and friendly contact by a personal representative of the association may result in a fairer treatment of our pictures within the proper limits of responsibility which the censorship authorities must discharge.

The letter concluded with an expression of trust in me, stating that I was 'particularly qualified for the mission'.

The problem of obtaining a normal, civilian passport was overcome by the fact that Hays knew Ruth Shipley, the head of the US State Department's passport division. A new passport was required because the one I had used in 1939 had to be surrendered on return from Europe in late July that year. Shipley responded favorably to a personal letter from Hays which explained how important it was for American films in Ireland that I should be able to go there and discuss issues with the film censor.

Once a US passport dated 28 November 1942 was received, it was possible to get on with the matter of obtaining an Irish visa. This too went well – at least in the initial stages. I had an introduction to Leo McCauley, Irish Consul General in New York. We lunched together and he guided me through the formalities at his office. My visa request required cable approval from Dublin, which was received quite promptly. The complications with respect to the Irish visa grew because it was valid for only six weeks. As my departure from the US was repeatedly delayed, it became necessary for me to get a series of extensions of the Irish visa, each requiring Consul General McCauley's personal signature. Before I finally left New York bound for Ireland in early May, there seemed to be no room for further extensions of the Irish visa.

Of all the obstacles on my road to service in neutral Ireland, the biggest one resulted from actions of the OSS's own security office. As incredible as it may seem, representatives of the security office came within a knife edge of blowing my cover.

It is of course obvious that the OSS, as a secret organisation carrying on delicate tasks under the direction of the American High Command, had to exercise extreme caution with respect to all its activities and have confidence in the trustworthiness of its personnel. Hence a security office was an essential function. However, in my case at least, one of the members of the staff was a grave security risk himself. Whether the individual acted in full deliberation, in ignorance or as personal revenge is an open question.

I had been accepted for OSS service following an interview with George K. Bowden, at that time a key associate of General Donovan, head of the OSS. My previous work and personal history were well known. Formal Security approval was granted to me on 26 December 1942. On 8 January 1943, A. van Beuren of the security office wrote in a memo to Bowden that additional confidential information 'confirms the fact that the subject's loyalty, ability and personal character are of the highest.'

What had happened was that two representatives of the OSS security office had interviewed one of my referees on the same day. They seem to have vied with each other in their eagerness to deny the validity of my cover story as a representative of the Motion Picture Producers & Distributors of America and even revealed that I was to represent the OSS in secret intelligence in Ireland.

This particular referee was Reverend Wilfrid Parsons SJ, formerly editor of the Jesuit weekly magazine *America* and Dean of the Georgetown University Graduate School in Washington, DC. As Father Parsons recounted the incidents, one day in early 1943 a man named Richardson telephoned for an appointment; shortly afterwards another man named

Collins called for the same purpose. Father Parsons made appointments for both men for the same day – one at one time and the other later.

Richardson revealed everything: he said that he was from the OSS, he discussed the role of the Hays office in setting up my cover and he revealed where I was going. Father Parsons was, of course, very surprised. I had told him the cover story, which he had believed completely.

Collins at first merely identified himself as an investigator for a government agency and said he was not free to reveal which one it was. After he had asked the same line of general questions about me as had been asked by Richardson, Father Parsons told him about the previous visit. Collins then said that Richardson had been fired the day before.

When I learned of these developments I wrote to Francis P. Miller, my OSS boss, as follows:

Father Parsons is a very reliable and discreet person. No damage has been done by the fact that he knows everything about this. Nevertheless, it is information that he would naturally prefer not to know and it is not pleasing to me that he or anyone else should be told the whole story while I keep stressing the cover story.

It seems to me that the first man, Richardson, is either stupid or interested in hurting the work. If he was fired, I hope some watch has been kept on him so that information he obtained is not widely disseminated.

For the purposes of this work I do not mind misleading persons but I do not like to invent or attempt to invent stories to cover up an investigation which seems to partake more of the nature of advertising or publicity than very delicate checking. What defense can one make when friends wonder why they have been misled when secret details are either directly or indirectly revealed to them by total strangers?

My letter concluded by pointing out that I was not objecting to investigation but only to the timing of it and the methods involved. 'Personally I am willing to accept whatever happens in the line of this work,' I said.

Miller then wrote to Whitney Shepardson, SI head, 'This is the most serious violation of security that has been called to my attention. It is particularly galling to reflect that in this case our security was destroyed by an alleged investigator of the security office.' He asked that General Donovan call for a report from the security office.

In retrospect, I can understand why it was so difficult – and took so long – to make arrangements to get an OSS undercover agent to Ireland. At the time I found it hard to comprehend. For obvious reasons, military transport by sea or air was ruled out. Travel in a convoy on a ship which included some civilian passengers was not an option because no assurance could be given that a convoy might not have to land in Northern Ireland. A journey from Northern Ireland to Éire by train, bus or car was out of the question.

For months I urged that travel by air be arranged because that was the most consistent with my film-industry cover. Executives and production people regularly travelled in that way.

In the prevailing war conditions there were only two

possible air services available to me: Pan American, which flew via Lisbon to Foynes, and American Export, via Bermuda. Air service under British control could not be considered, for security reasons.

My application for a Portuguese transit visa was supported by a letter from Carl E. Milliken, former Governor of the State of Maine and head of the foreign department of the Motion Picture Producers & Distributors of America. Eventually pressure was applied in Lisbon through managers of the branch offices of the major American film companies. By the time a visa was obtained three months later on 22 March 1943, as a film representative I hadn't a high enough priority to get on a plane.

In late February I was advised that the chances of departure within twenty-four hours were so good that I should renew the Irish visa. In early March my chance of flying directly (via American Export) vanished because of an internal controversy within the OSS. The counter-intelligence branch insisted on the available air priority to send personnel for service in London.

On 13 March 1943, Whitney H. Shepardson sent a memo to William J. Donovan, OSS chief, as follows:

> Knowing of your very special interest in Martin Quigley's mission, I am sure you will be concerned about a situation which has developed regarding transportation for him; in the light of which you will probably wish to take some action.
>
> In view of the delicacy of Martin's mission, and because of the bitter experiences that we have had arranging similar missions in the past, we have

determined in Martin's case we would avoid the slightest move which might later jeopardise his chances for success.

Since we were unwilling to bring official pressure, it has been proven impossible to secure a Portuguese visa, although we have been waiting for this since December. Some weeks ago we concluded that Martin must go direct to Foynes via American Export Airlines. On February 13, a travel request was filed for space on that route. We seem to be at the end of our resources to secure such space. Martin has been very patient, but it will obviously be extremely bad for his morale if he has to wait much longer, since we have been working to get him off for three months.

Would you be willing to intervene personally in order to get Martin off immediately?

Donovan decided that there was no way he could personally intervene that would not risk exposure of my commercial cover, so the wait continued through the winter of 1943.

In early April, Carter Nicholas, my immediate OSS superior in Washington, noted that I was still polite but was beginning to show signs of considerable strain from the five months spent waiting for transportation.

By now improved express steamer transportation had been established between New York and the British Isles. The *Queen Elizabeth,* which had been rushed to the US in an unfinished state at the outbreak of the war, had been completed, and it joined the older *Queen Mary* in providing swift Atlantic crossings.

The *Queen Elizabeth* and *Queen Mary* carried primarily

troops but also provided passage on each trip for hundreds of civilians of many different occupations, some governmental and some not. Orders finally came for me with the necessary tickets. I was issued with a gas mask and a steel helmet at the Brooklyn navy yard and told the day and time to board at the Cunard pier on the Hudson River: that pier was visible from my office in the Music Hall Building in Rockefeller Center.

At last I would be on my way, subject only to the sea's perils, which then, of course, included German U-boats. It was rumoured that Hitler had offered a special prize for any submarine skipper who sank one of the huge *Queen* liners. These fast ships sailed without escort, relying on their speed to elude the U-Boat packs lurking all across the Atlantic.

After the *Queen Elizabeth* sailed, Carter Nicholas sent a telegram to my father: 'Martin and Betty off today.' The *Queen Elizabeth* had a number of main-deck cabins into which civilian passengers were crowded. Officers had similar staterooms. For enlisted men the ship had bunk space for only half the number on board. Hence, half the men at any given time had nowhere to lie down. Civilians and officers could carry their life jackets. The enlisted men had to wear theirs all the time. As a result, making one's way to the two meals a day through hundreds of men crowded in all the corridors – with their life jackets on – was quite difficult. There was quite a smell as the days wore on.

My assigned space was in a starboard-side, main-deck cabin which, after the war, would be fitted out luxuriously for two first-class passengers, most often a married couple. Now in place of the normal furniture, five double bunks had been erected; these occupied almost all the floor space. We were relatively lucky, as only eight civilians were quartered in that cabin, leaving two bunks to be filled with everyone's luggage.

The *Queen Elizabeth* carried approximately 15,000 troops, perhaps as many as 500 civilians and a large ship's crew. The only real movement about the ship was to the two meals served daily. For our cabin, meals were at 10 am and 4 pm in the second-class dining room, far from our cabin, which was at the end of the ship.

We spent most of the time in our cabin lying on the bunks: there were no chairs. In the small space by the door, four or five of the men would often sit on the floor and play cards. I did not play but still remember one of the cabin-mates championing 'super-peculiar baseball poker'. I soon learned that six of the seven other men were from the Research and Analysis Branch of the OSS and had been assigned to work at the organisation's London office. The seventh, somewhat older than the rest, was a labour-relations specialist, also employed by the OSS.

Naturally I was unhappy that I had been put in a cabin with people who were not only US government employees but who worked for the OSS. This circumstance made it necessary for me to make sure that every one of my roommates was quickly convinced that I was not 'one of them' but was just a civilian representing the American motion-picture industry. Fortunately I was successful. Later I learned that one of them complained to his superior about the presence among government workers of a civilian.

Just after the *Queen Elizabeth* steamed out of New York harbour and passed Ambrose lightship, the liner was strafed by two planes, fortunately using blank ammunition. The effect – probably intended – was to terrify thousands of the soldiers, most of whom had never seen an ocean and did not know how to swim. It was a forceful reminder that this sea voyage was not a pleasure trip.

The passage was mercifully quick – only one day longer than the liner would take in peacetime runs. That extra day was due to a dramatic roll of the ship as the rudder was put hard over, presumably because a U-boat pack had been detected just ahead. The evasion manouvre added hundreds of miles to the crossing to Greenock, in Scotland. The sight of the British Sutherland flying boats on offshore patrol the next to last day out was greeted with great relief by all aboard. This meant air cover would be available for the rest of the trip. The last tense moments were when the *Queen Elizabeth* snaked through an extensive British minefield that was protecting the entrances to the port. While the calendar said May, the hills around the harbour were snow-capped. It was a welcome and most beautiful sight.

The first report of the trip to reach Francis Miller, my OSS boss in Washington, was a personal letter from Colonel R. Cresswell written in London on 20 May 1943:

You will be amused to know that your man, about whose passport such a row was raised, travelled on the same conveyance with me and is now staying at my hotel.

He has kept his cover admirably. He was put in the same stateroom with several R&A men, and apparently convinced all of them conclusively that he had no connection with the OSS. I am not sure whether or not he recognised me, but he has been very careful to give no sign of it so far.

I kept a fatherly eye on him during the trip, and afterwards on the train from the port of debarkation, of which I had command, because I knew that he must have gotten off in a frenzied hurry and because his apparent status was a very shaky one in military circles.

He strikes me as being unusually discreet and self-possessed, and I expect that he will do well.

The train, packed with troops and including a car or two of civilians, left Greenock station at dusk. There was no one in my compartment that I recognised from the boat; I was glad not to be travelling to London with the R&E OSS men. One brief stop was made at Edinburgh. There, for the first time, I saw Red Cross workers serving coffee and cakes to the soldiers leaning out of the windows of the train carriages.

The journey to London was slow and uneventful. There were no German air attacks that night along our route. The train arrived in London at about ten in the morning. Here I was in London and I thought then that I would finally be able to begin work in Ireland within a day or two. I was wrong again.

The first thing I had to do was find a place to stay. Hotel rooms were scarce in wartime London. Fortunately a phone call from the station to the office of my father's publishing company connected me with Hope Williams Burnup, the manager. Universally known as 'Hopie', she had hundreds of friends. Her first husband, J. D. Williams, founded the first film studios in England at Elstree. After his death she was an assistant to Samuel L. 'Roxy' Rothafel, for whom the movie palace at Seventh Avenue and Fiftieth Street in New York City was named. In 1937 she returned to her native England to open a small office for Quigley Publishing Company. Her second husband was Peter Burnup, then war correspondent for the mass-circulation British weekly newspaper the *News of the World*.

With a call to the manager of the Park Lane Hotel, Hopie Burnup obtained a room reservation for me. The rest of the day was spent complying with wartime regulations. As a foreigner, I had to register at a nearby police station. Then, with a trip to the other section of London, I had to obtain a food ration book. Also, I checked in at the office of Fay Allport, London manager for the Motion Picture Producers & Distributors of America, but found he was out of town.

When I visited Ireland's passport and visa office in London the next day, I got the astonishing news that the visa issued and renewed repeatedly by the Irish Consulate General's office in New York City was not valid for travel between England and Dublin on account of a recent change in the regulations. It was only good for entrance directly from the US by plane to Foynes on the Shannon (as I had originally intended) or directly by boat from the States – but there was no such sea service. Finally there was an agreement to check with the Foreign Office in Dublin for instructions, as my case seemed quite unique.

After a week without a response, I decided to call Dublin myself. From our publishing company's office at 4 Golden Square, I made a phone call to Walter McNally, the RKO Radio Pictures manager for Ireland and a cinema owner (and a family friend whom I had met in 1933 and 1939). I was never told to whom McNally spoke, but the okay to validate my New York-issued visa was received in the Irish office the next day.

Were my problems with red tape over? Not at all. When I sought an exit permit at British passport control, I was told my US passport was good only for travel to the North and could not be used for Ireland. This situation necessitated a visit to the American Embassy so that it could be explained to the British authorities that the US State Department did not use the word 'Éire' in validating passports but just the word 'Ireland' to cover both sections of the island.

So after a telegram to McNally and a gift to our London office of my steel helmet and gas mask, the next day I finally made it to Dublin via the London–Holyhead train and the ferry to Dun Laoghaire.

I was just five months later than originally intended. I thought to myself: better late than never!

3

Hazards of the Job

As the ferry docked at Dun Laoghaire I saw on the quay Walter McNally with his flowing bow tie. The ship was quite crowded but the debarkation was rapid. The Irish customs and immigration lines moved smoothly. There was no problem with the visa issued in New York, and I was given a visitor's permit that was good for three months.

Since he did not drive, McNally had his driver take us on the short trip to the Shelbourne Hotel in Dublin. I had only one medium-size bag. On registration I was given a small single bedroom with one window overlooking St Stephen's Green. A second window was in a bathroom which had been carved out of the room. That was my room whenever I was in Dublin. I would give it up during my trips to provincial cities and towns and for the month I was in London, but on returning to the Shelbourne I was always assigned to the same room. The price uniformly was one pound per night. I always had breakfast in the Shelbourne dining room and often had lunch there, usually with a guest from the entertainment or media world.

As I began my intelligence mission it seemed appropriate to review in my mind the hazards I was facing. They fell into both general and specific categories, the general ones occasioned by the war situation in the spring of 1943 and those concerning health and safety which travellers face at all times. The specific hazards arose from potential threats to my cover from a number of sources.

The war situation in Europe remained grim. The Nazis were still threatening an invasion of Britain. Cities and towns throughout the British Isles were subjected to nightly air raids. London was soon to be a target of long-range missiles. France was a German puppet country. Mussolini in Italy followed Hitler's orders. German armies were deep inside Soviet Russia. On the other side of the world, Japanese forces held almost all of East Asia and were threatening Australia. In north Africa the Allies were in bitter conflict with the German Afrika Corps.

In Ireland the number of believers in a Nazi victory or an eventual stalemate was decreasing but was still substantial. Northern Ireland was rapidly becoming a major training area for American ground troops preparing for an eventual invasion of the German-held Continent. These troops were forbidden to visit any part of the twenty-six counties.

The prevailing military opinion in both London and Washington at this time was that any Nazi invasion attempt against Britain would be accompanied by – or preceded by a day or two by – an invasion of neutral Ireland. The aim of this would be to cut air and sea communications between Britain and the New World.

Had there been such a German invasion, my plan was to go to ground with friends near Carlow. My family had lived for many hundreds of years in farmlands around Timahoe in County Laois. Even though my grandparents had emigrated to the United States a century before at the time of the Great Famine, a change out of American clothes would make an Irishman of me, at least in appearance. I would then turn from collecting essentially political intelligence to gathering military intelligence. For communication with the OSS, I would rely on radio equipment dropped in with the inevitable Allied counter-thrust to a Nazi invasion of Ireland.

I was fortunate that during my stay in Ireland I had no travel or other accidents and enjoyed fine health: I was never sick or even inconvenienced by a cold or an ache. That I had lost a good deal of weight came to my attention when I was sent a print of a snapshot of me taken on a visit to Waterford. Although I was normally thin in those days (an OSS superior the following year dubbed me 'the Thin Man'), I consulted a doctor in Dublin, who confirmed that my health was excellent. My loss of more than twenty pounds in weight in a short time was attributed to the available diet. The Shelbourne and other good hotels and restaurants were suffering the effects of wartime shortages, as were the Irish people generally. The doctor prescribed a pint of Guinness daily.

The major particular hazards I had to reckon with came from the various security and counter-intelligence services. First mention needs to be made of the Irish. No country wants secret intelligence carried on within its borders by another country. My work, of course, was illegal from the point of view of the Irish government. I was a potential target at any time of the Garda Síochána or members of army intelligence.

One morning after I had finished breakfast at my usual table near the entrance of the Shelbourne's dining room, I received word from the reception desk that a garda wished to talk to me. I asked that he come up to my room. The young man was dressed in civilian clothes so I never knew whether he was a garda detective or a member of army intelligence. He was soft-spoken and polite, with the apparent mission of verifying who I was and what I was doing in Dublin. He left fifteen or twenty minutes later, convinced that I was doing what I said I was doing, after being told more than he probably wanted to know about the workings of the Film Censor Office and the troubles of American film distributors in Ireland.

The only other known contact with the gardai or intelligence occurred when I was leaving early one morning after a few days spent in Tralee. I had stayed at Benner's Hotel, across the street from the cinema operated by Mr & Mrs Patrick Coffey. The Coffeys had been long-time subscribers to the weekly film trade journal *Motion Picture Herald*, published by my father. Despite the severe petrol rationing, they took me on an afternoon drive to see some of the beautiful land along the River Shannon. While waiting on the railway-station platform for the one train that day to Kilkenny, I happened to notice a man attempting to conceal himself behind a phone booth. Since there were only a few persons waiting – the others obviously locals – I assumed at the time, perhaps wrongly, that the man was a detective assigned to verify that I actually left Tralee.

Many years after the war, Colonel Dan Brian, then in charge of Irish intelligence and counter-intelligence, said, 'Quigley's cover was perfect. We did not know he was OSS.'

Shortly before I had left New York on the *Queen Elizabeth*, the OSS Irish Desk Officer, Carter Nicholas, discussed with Hugh R. Wilson, a high official of the US State Department in Washington, what the effects of the uncovering of an OSS agent in Ireland might be. (That, of course, meant me because I was the only OSS agent in Ireland under cover, a fact I did not know until after the war.)

Wilson responded for the State Department: 'Even though Mr de Valera might attempt to make political capital out of such a circumstance [the uncovering of an OSS agent], it would not worry the State Department. The State Department believes that the Irish-Americans feel ashamed of their country's position and would not be offended by evidence of OSS activities in Ireland.'

Should I be so unlucky as to be revealed as an American intelligence agent, I felt it would be an embarrassing situation that was likely to become something of an international incident. Very likely de Valera would have made a strong objection to the US State Department and had me expelled. In the circumstances I had no fear that a failure would result in a long jail sentence or worse.

A break in my cover was likely to cause even more problems with the British than with the Irish. The British government has from time immemorial considered Ireland a private preserve in intelligence matters and it wanted no American undercover activity in Ireland. After the war I learned that the head of the OSS intelligence branch, Whitney Shepardson, thought at one time there was an agreement that the OSS would respect the wish of the British government in this regard and not have any undercover intelligence in Ireland. In any event – lower-level agreement or not – Donovan, the head of the OSS, specifically authorised and monitored my undercover mission. It was a case where British and US viewpoints did not coincide.

A discovery of my true intelligence role – whether by the Irish or by the British official or unofficial representatives in Éire – would have been seized upon by the British 'to raise holy hell', with the possible compromising of the OSS - British intelligence cooperation in many areas and fields of activity. It also would have been an embarrassment to Will H. Hays, the Motion Picture Producers & Distributors of America, Inc. and the member film companies, especially their branch managers in Dublin.

Another potentially serious threat to my work in Ireland was the spreading of a rumour that I was a British intelligence agent. The chance of this happening was probably slim but someone might identify me as a foreigner – in Dublin or more likely in a provincial town – and jump to the erroneous conclusion that I was, or might be, a British secret intelligence agent. Secret British agents have long been part of Irish history; few unaware of the background would suspect that the US government would be employing undercover agents in any part of Ireland.

Another area of concern was the diplomats and other nationals (including likely intelligence officers) of Germany, Italy and Japan. My basic policy was to avoid calling undue attention to myself. As far as I know, the Axis nationals made only one direct attempt to check up on me. Presumably, if my work as a representative of the American film industry working on war-related censorship matters came to their attention (as it probably did), my bona fides would be accepted.

The exception was on a visit to Cork. I was staying at

the hotel there that is famed for not serving alcoholic beverages. When I was out of my room one day attending a lunch of cinema managers, my bag was searched. How did I know that? One of the lessons learned in OSS training was a simple method of making sure you knew whether your bag had been searched, but the person who searched it could not detect that your bag had been 'armed' against such an action.

Previously I had noted at my hotel the presence of two Japanese nationals, who were presumably members of their small diplomatic mission. It is of course possible that someone else went through my bag. However, since nothing was taken, the perpetrator was not looking for anything of monetary value. If my bag had been searched by or for the Japanese, what was found would only confirm my cover profession. I always packed papers that would substantiate my work as an American film industry official.

I had also been instructed to make sure that neither David Gray, American Minister, nor any member of his US legation staff ever learned that I was a member of the OSS on an undercover intelligence mission. The reasons for this were several. Prior to my arrival in Ireland, two OSS representatives had been attached to the Dublin American Legation. Neither was actually undercover; both had official US passports. Minister Gray was not happy about the blending of diplomatic and intelligence work.

Gray had an unusual status for the American Minister in a relatively small country. (In those days, Ireland had not been elevated to the status of having the American representative titled 'Ambassador' heading an Embassy rather than a Legation.) He was married to an aunt of Eleanor Roosevelt, the President's wife. He would often go outside the official channels of communication through the State Department and write 'Dear Franklin' letters directly to President Roosevelt at the White House.

That might have been an advantage for all concerned except that Gray had such poor personal relations with de Valera that he was virtually cut off from him at times and was without good contacts with other officials of the Irish government. Moreover, it was felt in some quarters in Washington that he was too close to the Anglo-Irish commercial interests and the Protestant community in general. His social contacts did not include 'the common people' or their opinion-makers and leaders.

Shortly after I arrived in Dublin, I made a courtesy call on Minister Gray at the American Legation. This was in keeping with my role as a representative of the Motion Picture Producers & Distributors of America. We talked about Will Hays, whom Gray knew favourably by reputation as well as for his support of the severe film censorship which had banned some Hollywood films and mutilated others. He said he would like to present me to de Valera but unfortunately he was leaving shortly on a trip to the United States. I concealed my delight at this. Gray was the last person I wanted to be with when I was talking with de Valera. And yet it's only fair to say that I found David Gray – his views about de Valera and Irish matters generally notwithstanding – a brave and honorable man. 'Should the Germans invade Ireland,' he told me, 'I plan to take up a position here at the Embassy gate with rifle in hand and resist the Nazis as long as I am alive.'

The most important factor, so far as preservation of my

commercial cover was concerned, was Dr Richard Hayes, the official film censor. Had he any doubts about me or my capability of working with him in an unobjectionable manner, my opportunity of serving in Ireland would have been terminated, perhaps abruptly. My work there certainly could not have endured for half a year.

Dr Hayes was a gentleman of the old school in the very best sense of the term. Trained as a medical doctor, he was serious and soft-spoken. His Irish Revolution credentials were impeccable and of the highest order. He had been active in his medical capacity in the Easter Rebellion of 1916. He was captured by the British and served time in English prisons along with de Valera, Michael Collins, and other well-known Irish patriots.

A significant part of Hayes's life had been devoted to historical research. His writings on the 'Flight of the Earls' and the story of the huge numbers of Irishmen who fought and died in the armies of France for three centuries following exile after the Battle of Limerick are classics.

As the film censor he was meticulous and conscientious. After our first meeting, I was pleased that Dr Hayes invited me to sit beside him as he screened movies almost every weekday morning. The censor's office was in an old building on Molesworth Street, not far from the Dáil. At the film screenings Dr Hayes sat at a desk on a raised platform behind a table with a small lamp. A copy of the script of the film was open on the table so he could make cuts, looking back and forth from the screen to the script.

I was given ample opportunity to discuss Dr Hayes's cuts with him. On a few rare occasions, after listening to my observations, he eliminated or shortened a few of the cuts. I fear my presence made an already difficult job even more so. He was on sure ground in dealing with his own ideas of what censorship on moral grounds should be. I did not always agree but I was not there to debate moral issues but rather wartime censorship under the Emergency Powers Act. While there was an Appeal Board to which a film distributor could go to seek a review of Dr Hayes's decisions, such appeals were rarely successful. I never participated in any aspect of the appeal process.

I tried – not very successfully – to have allowed in films as much about the war as was regularly permitted in the press. (The public knew all about war developments from listening to the BBC radio broadcasts.) On one occasion Dr Hayes wanted to cut a whole scene in a New York City business office which had nothing to do with the war because on the wall there was visible a poster with the slogan 'Buy War Bonds'. Another time he wanted to cut an incidental bit of dialogue: 'While you know there is a war on.'

The greatest problem for Dr Hayes in the period I was in Ireland occurred when he approved with minor cuts the film *A Yank in the RAF.* After it had played a whole week at the Savoy on O'Connell Street, it was 'yanked' – banned on the direct order of Frank Aiken, Minister for the Co-ordination of Defensive Measures. I could not resist complaining to Archbishop Pascal Robinson, the Papal Nuncio to Ireland, when a two-reel short subject titled 'Army Chaplain' was banned. The film showed a Catholic priest helping a Jewish soldier die.

Every contact I made constituted a potential threat to a break in the security of my cover. This applied especially to members of the press, who by nature tend to be suspicious.

The potential existed with everyone I met, be they branch managers of the distributing companies, exhibitors, parish priests and other clergy or just ordinary people. One film manager remarked to me, after I had been in Ireland several weeks, 'I thought at first that you must be some kind of government representative – perhaps for the British government. But now I know you're not – you're just representing the American film industry. I hope you succeed in obtaining some relaxation of the film censorship. I doubt that you will, but I wish you luck.'

What made my cover a good one was that I was fully competent to do what I said I was doing. I did the cover job for many of my working hours every day. The only weakness in my position was that someone really knowledgeable about the economics of the American and British film industry might question the need to send someone to Ireland for a period of months to negotiate with the Irish film censor. The Irish film market was a very small part of the British market and a tiny part of the world market for Hollywood films. My defence against this possible suspicion was to stress as often as seemed appropriate that while no single American motion picture company would wish to incur such expense, the association composed of the eight major film-producing firms thought it worthwhile for financial reasons, for improvement of public relations and because the proportional cost to each company would be small. The public relations aspect had to be considered because Americans of Irish origin lived mainly in or around major cities, where the greatest part of the film industry's box-office receipts were obtained. Irish-Americans were great movie-goers. There was a concern that withholding US films from Ireland – which was a real possibility given the bans and cuts of the Emergency Powers censorship – would generate press attention that would disturb Irish-American movie audiences. I would also point out that the American film industry was mindful of the growing numbers of US troops being trained in Northern Ireland for an eventual invasion of Nazi-held Europe. Those troops were not allowed to visit Ireland but it was felt that news of a withdrawal of American films from Ireland would be sure to reach them and might have a poor public relations effect on Americans of Irish origin among them.

It was clearly important that I get some feel of the sentiments of the IRA. At this time the de Valera government had interned a number of militant members of the IRA for fear they might show displeasure with government policies by terrorist attacks or other violent means. In view of my cover, I had to proceed very cautiously. I passed the word to an acquaintance that I would like to speak to a member of the IRA who could enlighten me about the organisation's film policy.

Some time before I had arrived in Dublin, several IRA men had broken into the projection booth of a first-run Dublin theatre on O'Connell Street, taken several reels of film at gunpoint and thrown them into the Liffey. This gave me a justification for looking into the film policy of the IRA.

A few days after I had extended the invitation, I received a phone call from a young man who did not give me his name. I invited him to my hotel room and we had a cordial visit for about an hour. At its end, I felt sure that the IRA was not about to open a campaign against American films.

Unsuspected by my visitor, I believe, I was able to learn a good deal about IRA attitudes on other matters.

One Sunday I had taken the tram from Dublin to Dun Laoghaire to visit the widowed sister of Mae Slocock, an Irish woman and wife of Viv Slocock, a trainer of polo ponies in Pinehurst, North Carolina. I was taken to meet a neighbour's family. Their name was Harte. My basic OSS code name – selected by me months before at the OSS's secret farm in Virginia – was Harte. I trust there was no expression of surprise when I was introduced to the Hartes.

Another secret name I had chosen – a random group of five letters to be used only in cables – was NALSI. That was never employed because, quite obviously, there was no way I could send coded cables from Ireland, given my cover status.

During my half-year in Ireland I risked being in a compromising situation should someone (such as a maid) come unannounced into my hotel room. The double-transposition code system was sufficiently complex that I felt that I should test the coding process after I had been out of the US for several months. I did not want to be in the position of having forgotten an essential step if the unlikely necessity to send a coded message to the OSS came about. So I made up a message, did the double transposition and wrote out the results in the prescribed five-letter groups. I had satisfied myself that I remembered my lines of poetry and the double transposition system. But how would I get rid of the work papers and the manuscript code message? My solution was (appropriately) out of a B-movie. I tore up the papers into tiny pieces and flushed them down the toilet. My first and last coding in Ireland!

In case of emergency I had been given in Washington a

means of identifying myself to an individual at the American legation. I was to ask this question: 'Do you happen to know where the Gallow Glasses originated?' The answer was to be: 'The Hebrides.' It was fortunate that no emergency arose, as the individual who did not know my identity until many years later had left Ireland before I got there.

The instructions given me by my OSS superior had allowed me great freedom of operation. They included the following:

Your territory is Ireland. You will not be the only OSS representative in Ireland but you will not report to, be responsible to or be subordinate to any other representative there.

You will go to Dublin as the representative of the Motion Picture Producers and Distributors of America, Inc, to carry on continuing negotiations with respect to the Irish censorship of American films, to make study of films which in the past have been found objectionable to the censorship authorities and to the people of Ireland and to advise the association on how trouble may be avoided in the future. This work will continue for a considerable period, perhaps as long as a year.

It would be well for you to confine yourself in the beginning very carefully to the direct and pressing interests of the association. You will be expected to move slowly and cautiously with your work for this office [the OSS].

'What was a single young American man doing in a civilian film job in Ireland in the midst of the war?' and 'Why wasn't he in some branch of the US military?' were questions likely to be asked. They were asked once, at an interview I had with Archbishop Joseph McQuaid. The archbishop resolved the matter himself, noting that he appreciated the importance of censorship to the American film industry. After that observation, he reached across his desk, picked up his telephone and called Joseph Walshe, the Minister for Foreign Affairs, to make an appointment for me to see him.

If anyone looked into the military service questions, the 'paper trail' would explain the situation. While the glasses I wore made it obvious that I was very near-sighted, it was on the record that I had been classified 4-F (unfit for military service) by the Draft Board in Greenwich, Connecticut, many months before I was sworn in as a member of the OSS. The National Office of the Selective Service in Washington, DC, eventually instructed the Greenwich Draft Board to leave my status unchanged and grant me permission to travel abroad to 'Confidential' countries for 'Confidential' work. Naturally there was nothing on that record to show a connection with the OSS.

A draft of my instructions in the winter of 1943 included some topics in the area of strictly military intelligence. Any investigations by me on these topics would have been inconsistent with my film cover and likely to lead to the discovery of my espionage role. The authorities at OSS headquarters realised the inconsistency of having an agent under commercial cover dig into military affairs, and my orders were amended.

My final orders were phrased in a lengthy series of

questions to which I should seek answers. The first group of questions dealt with attitudes: 'What is the true attitude of the Irish government towards the US? towards US troops in Northern Ireland? towards Germany and the other Axis powers? What is the power of the Roman Catholic hierarchy in Ireland? What is the attitude of the Catholic hierarchy in Ireland with regard to Germany and the US?'

Other questions concerned the effectiveness of propaganda directed at the Irish people, the IRA and its attitudes, the attitudes of labour unions and labour leaders and communications of various types.

I was pleased that my instructions included the following, which further removed me from characterization as a typical spy: 'You are not to hire subagents for undercover work.'

The final section of my orders reflected the background of Francis Miller as a distinguished Virginian:

It is well to remember that it will increase the efficiency of your work if you will go on your way quietly instead of throwing your weight around. Refrain from cultivating contacts with the representatives of other American services in your territory such as Army, Navy, State Department, etc., but when your path naturally crosses theirs (in normal social relations, for example), deport yourself so that you may enlist their sympathy, aid, and friendship. In cases where this is not possible, avoid the individual concerned as much as you can.

Mr Miller's last words in the formal orders were:

> The methods of carrying out your negotiations with
> Dr Hayes or his successor in office or with Frank
> Aiken or his successor, your travel within Ireland, your
> contacts with the Irish people, and your manner of
> performing your cover job and your OSS job are a
> responsibility in general within your sole discretion.
> You have been selected to carry out this important,
> delicate and difficult mission because we trust your
> discretion and your ability, upon which the success or
> failure of your mission almost entirely depends.

4

An End to Partition?

My mission was essentially the gathering of strategic intelligence: information, data, impressions, attitudes, actions and beliefs that broadened the understanding of those for whom the material was being prepared. The wartime role of the OSS's strategic-intelligence branch, of which I was a member, was to provide decision-makers with information which would help them make appropriate decisions.

As I have already noted, I was an independent intelligence agent (spy, if you will) in a country where none of my OSS superiors was resident. Once I left the United States I could not be given additional orders or even guidance. I was literally on my own.

I was at liberty to come and go as I wished in wartime Ireland and to do what I thought would best advance the aims of the OSS and the United States' national interests generally. The only operational restriction was that I was not to engage subagents. That suited me, since that kind of espionage practice was inconsistent with the film-industry cover and because such contacts are a threat to secrecy. As the old adage (attributed to the Sicilian mafia) puts it: 'Three men can keep a secret – when two of them are dead.'

After several months in Ireland I came to realise that the partition of the island, imposed in 1921, was the dominant political condition. Partition meant that six of the nine counties of Ulster were cut off from the other twenty-six counties and retained their status as part of the United Kingdom. The other counties formed the Irish Free State in a Commonwealth association with Great Britain. Partition was a condition that cast a cloud reaching into the indefinite future.

Much of the thought about the war from a military viewpoint in Éire, as the Irish Free State was then called, and in Britain was the status of the treaty ports of military bases in Ireland handed over by the British government to the government of Éire in 1938, just a year before the Germans launched World War II by invading Poland and Danzig.

I formulated a plan: lend the Irish bases not back to the British but to the Americans. In exchange, obtain the promise of the United States government to use its best efforts to secure the end of Partition when the war with the Axis powers was over.

A minority tradition of advocacy of separatism had long existed in parts of Ulster. There were discussions on this subject in London during World War I. Partition as voted by the British House of Parliament in 1921, however, flowed from the Easter Rising of 1916, the ensuing Anglo-Irish War and the protracted Treaty negotiations. It was the major cause of the Irish Civil War.

A key player in the crucial years following the 1916 Rising through the establishment of the Irish Free State and into World War II was the IRA.

The origin of Partition cannot be understood without an appreciation of the forces that brought the IRA into being and provided its motivation. The IRA has gone through various phases in the years since the name was given to volunteers in 1917. Or, more accurately, several divergent and distinct groups have claimed and used the title and its initials for different purposes. At the time of the 'troubles' of the Anglo-Irish War (January 1919 to July 1921), the IRA was the rallying point of resistance to British rule; in later times the IRA became an illegal terror organisation.

From the Irish point of view, the old or original IRA had a glorious record. Many of the men prominent in public life during World War II had been active members of the first IRA. In Easter week of 1916, members of earlier military organisations made several brave but hopeless stands against British forces. The Irish leaders were all sentenced to execution, but some, including Éamon de Valera and Michael Collins, had their sentences commuted to jail terms and were subsequently released or escaped.

When Irish military action was used to counter the brutality of the British 'Black and Tan' forces, the IRA was the main body of attack. It was organised on military lines, with a general staff, but considered itself merely the armed service of the rightful government of the Republic of Ireland. Members of the IRA were devoted, perhaps fanatical, patriots and were skilled in all forms of guerrilla warfare.

One typical story of the reaction to the search for facts about the Anglo-Irish War tells how a small group of English journalists arranged for an interview in Dublin with a high-ranking IRA official. When they were finally conducted to a small, bare room and met the leader, they put to him the question, 'Tell us what all this is about.' The newspapermen, settling back into their chairs, expected a statement of considerable length. They were astonished when the IRA man said one thing and nothing more: 'Revenge, by God!'

A vignette of the period is given by Joseph M. Stanley, motion picture theatre operator and publisher of the *Drogheda Argus* and, in the times of the 'troubles,' printer and propagandist for revolutionists. On one occasion a group of IRA men threw a bomb into a British lorry as it rolled by Nelson's Pillar in Dublin's O'Connell Street. There was an old woman standing by the pillar selling fruit. 'Two oranges a penny. Two oranges a penny.' The British army lorry approached; the IRA men tossed their bomb. The woman instinctively fell flat on the pavement. The noise of the bomb died down, as did the crack of several rifle shots replying from the lorry. The woman picked herself up, dusted off her dress, and resumed her chant, 'Two oranges a penny. Two oranges a penny.' The peddler had never even glanced at the lorry and was quite unruffled by the incident. And so, much of Irish life continued during the 'troubles,' ignoring them when possible.

A basic and fundamental difficulty of the IRA appeared in 1921, when the British offered an armistice and negotiations for a peace treaty. A majority of the representatives in the legislature accepted the treaty and the Irish Free Sate was formed. A dissident group of the IRA, however, accused those who had accepted the treaty as being traitors to the ideals of the Irish Republic and to the many old and recent Irish 'martyrs'. De Valera led the section which held out for an absolute republic and waged war against the Free State, whose armed forces were led by Michael Collins, acting head of the Irish Free State.

As it became increasingly clear that the IRA's struggle against the 'Free Staters' was hopeless and that the Civil War was only further ruining the country, many members of the IRA gave up and retired to peaceful pursuits. The death in an ambush of Collins saddened those on both sides in the war.

In May 1923 almost all the IRA members decided to suspend violence. De Valera and a number of his colleagues eventually accepted seats in the Dáil, the representative assembly of the Irish Free State.

Once the Irish Free State had been established, it was obvious that a body of laws was immediately necessary. An act was passed in the Dáil which provided for continuation of the full range of British laws. Except as modified or increased by specific Irish bills, nothing was or has been done about changing regulations which, when administered by the British, were considered oppressive.

When de Valera became head of the Irish Free State in 1932, a number of members of his old branch of the IRA seemed to have expected him to break off relations with England and renew the fight for an Irish Republic, but de Valera had evidently decided that Ireland could achieve through peaceful means about all that could be reasonably expected at this period in her history. His administration seemed to look no more kindly on the extreme IRA that he had led than did the Cosgrave administration, which in its first years waged war against the IRA.

In the new constitution of 1937, framed by de Valera, many of Ireland's apparent ties with England were cut. The Irish Free State was abolished and the creation of Éire, or Ireland, was proclaimed. The British government took no action as it held that no essential change had been made in the status of the country. The constitution claimed jurisdiction over the whole of Ireland but recognised that for the moment its sway was limited to the territory previously known as the Irish Free State. It claimed that Ireland was a free and independent nation but it acknowledged that it was linked for external affairs with the British Commonwealth of Nations. The British government continued to regard Ireland as it had the Free State – as a self-governing dominion.

The old guard of the IRA at length lost patience with their former leader and adopted a new, illegal, terrorist campaign. In the early part of 1939, the IRA, which had attracted new blood from unemployed youths – and some money from America – declared war on England! This act was allegedly done in the name of the Irish Republic government. The legality of the Irish Free State and the Irish governments was denied by the IRA..

The new IRA launched a campaign which has so damaged its name that it is likely to go down in history on a very black page. Indiscriminate and terrorist bombings were inaugurated in the North of Ireland and in England. Arms were seized from Irish authorities. A number of people, including women and children, were killed. England was forced to take extraordinary precautions. During the summer of 1939 people entering public buildings or museums were searched, purses and parcels were examined and railway terminals and places of assembly were guarded.

This IRA bombing campaign aroused no sympathy. The Irish people and their leaders were deeply grieved. Relations with England were sharply strained. The bad effects on public opinion the world over were incalculable.

During this war the de Valera government found it necessary to take strict measures against the IRA. Active members were rounded up and interned in the Curragh military camp, where they were kept until they agreed to refrain from illegal action. Some hundreds were still locked up after four years of the war in Europe; a smaller number had been released. Others, convicted of criminal acts, were in regular jails.

As the people in Ireland feared to give testimony, especially in a case where physical harm might come to them, the Irish government turned over the trials of alleged members of 'illegal organisations' (meaning usually the new IRA) to military courts, which have the power to impose the death penalty. Hunger strikes have resulted.

Nevertheless, the continued existence of the spirit that has motivated the IRA from its establishment must be taken into consideration in connection with Partition. In fact, the actions of the IRA – under whatever sponsorship – cannot be understood historically without an appreciation of the causes and effects of Partition.

Ireland's gravest internal problem for the past twenty-five years has been Partition. In 1921, when the border was set up between the two sections of Ireland, Partition may have seemed to some as an excellent political expedient which avoided settling the basic questions. In effect it reminds one of Solomon's decision about the disposition of a baby claimed by two women – but in this case an arm was cut off from the rest of the body. Naturally, the wound has not and probably never will heal by itself.

The Partition of Ireland, adopted by the British government even though it did not win the vote of a single Irish member of the House of Parliament from Ulster or elsewhere, did not create all the present problems but it did aggravate many of them. Northern Ireland for centuries has in many respects developed in ways distinct from the rest of the country. There, the industrial revolution met with great success. Factories, mills and a shipbuilding industry were established, while most of the rest of Ireland remained essentially agricultural.

Another important historical factor is that the 'plantations' in Ireland were more widespread and their effect more lasting in Ulster than in the other provinces. From the time of the Irish chieftain, Hugh O'Neill, in Queen Elizabeth's day, Scottish settlers were forcibly established in Ulster. The natives were Catholics; the newcomers were Protestants. The latter took over the land and wealth of the area and to a major extent still hold them today.

The original idea in 1921 had apparently been to apply Woodrow Wilson's concept of self-determination to a particular segment of the island of Ireland. But on examination of the actual situation in Ireland, no community was believed sufficiently large to support itself, even with the assistance of British subsidies. So to the four counties of Ireland in which there were a majority of Unionists, or people who favored British rule, there were added two adjoining counties. Even then, only six of the ancient nine counties of Ulster were included. Had all nine been incorporated into Northern Ireland there would have been a more even balance of power between Protestants and Catholics.

The problem of the Partition of Ireland, if viewed objectively and calmly, is a difficult one to solve. If approached with passion and prejudice, it is and will remain nothing short of impossible.

There are actually five aspects of the question: religious, economic, political, cultural and strategic. In the beginning, religious differences naturally fanned strife in Ireland, but other considerations were of more real importance. Religion was – and still is – used as a label to conceal factors that are essentially economic. Protestants have the economic wealth and power in Northern Ireland; Catholics are the less-skilled workers and are also represented largely in the unemployed. That is a general statement and there are, of course, exceptions.

The Industrial Revolution did not create in Northern Ireland a condition which provided full employment in normal times. There was great competition for jobs. There was also a fear that the industrial towns of the North would be dominated by the agricultural South. The Protestants of Ulster wanted to run their own affairs, essentially for economic reasons. Under the cloak of religious zeal for the status quo and a continuous appeal to sectarian prejudice, membership in the Protestant Orangemen served as a basis for allocating jobs in a narrow labour market.

From a political point of view, Partition is an excellent source of jobs. There must be border guards, customs inspectors, and numerous other positions which would not exist if there were one government for the whole island. If there were no Partition, there would be no Northern Ireland Parliament, and naturally these officials attempt to further entrench themselves and vigorously resist any attempts to end the border. A very important consideration is that the British government subsidises the Northern Ireland government.

The cultural differences between the North and South are at present relatively slight, allowing only for the large Scottish influence in the North, but one of the main projects of the de Valera administration and the previous Cosgrave administration in Ireland was the introduction of the Irish language. The people in the North who trade with London and other English centres cannot understand the reasons for the Irish-language campaign. Its success would tend to perpetuate Partition, despite the fact that the Irish government's prime objective is to end it.

The strategic factor is one to which those who partitioned Ireland may have given little thought but which is of fundamental importance today. So far as tomorrow is concerned, it may be the most serious point from the view of London, or even of Washington. The events of World War II showed that a country must control nearby areas which might otherwise serve as bases for enemy attacks. The English (and the Irish) would certainly not want Ireland to be another Crete on which some hostile power might descend from the air, occupy and from there lay siege to England, blocking the main supply routes to and from the New World.

As long as England has military bases in the North of Ireland it may not need them in the South, but it would seem to require them, or their equivalent, somewhere in Ireland and for an indefinite period. So while the original reasons for setting up Partition may have been economic and political, considerations for holding some ties with Ireland now are strategic. This does not mean that the English statesmen and politicians after World War I did not realise the strategic value of Ireland, but the progress of aerial warfare has shown in a new light the strategic importance of that island.

In the early years of World War II, when the Germans overran Poland and then bypassed the Maginot Line in France and drove the British forces off the Continent at Dunkirk, the Churchill government was desperate for any possible military assistance. German U-boats were taking a terrible toll in the Atlantic and the possible future extent of American aid was unknown. It is not surprising that under these circumstances there were not only general calls for Ireland to declare war on the Axis powers but specific calls for the return to Britain of the so-called Treaty ports or Irish bases.

In one instance, Winston Churchill, stunned by criticism in the House of Commons of shipping losses, using fiery words attributed these losses to the fact that his government did not have use of the old Irish naval bases. From the military point of view, the use of the great harbour at Cork, for example, would shorten lines of communication, bringing Allied sea power hundreds of miles closer to major Nazi submarine operational areas than from ports in England and Wales.

By 1943 the war situation had changed. Now the Germans were becoming increasingly concerned about defending their 'Fortress Europe' by making plans to resist an Anglo-American invasion. Fortifications of various kinds were being erected on the beaches and sea coasts of France and Belgium.

Large numbers of US troops were in training camps in Northern Ireland. In Ireland there was no longer a fear – or much of one – that the Nazis would invade the island or would ultimately win the war. A fight to the death was coming but no one knew how long it would take to begin. An Allied invasion of continental Europe could be expected and would, if successful, lead to final victory. But at that time, no one – from General Dwight Eisenhower down — could be certain that an invasion would be successful.

The war in Europe lasted two more years. From the perspective of 1943 it might have been thought that it would last many more.

In these circumstances the use of the treaty ports – or at least one of them, Cobh – might well have been of military value to the Allies. Cobh is the best natural harbor in the British Isles and one of the best in the world. Unlike the prevalent situation in the earlier years of the war, an abundance of war material was being produced in American factories. In the south Pacific, the United States was demonstrating the ability of its engineers to build air fields almost overnight. An American air base in County Cork would provide the shortest flying distance from fields in the New World.

Little possibility existed that the de Valera government would consent in 1943 to a transfer of the treaty ports back to Britain. After all, they had been given up very reluctantly in 1921 as part of the treaty ending the Anglo-Irish War. They had been returned to control by Ireland only five years ago, in 1938. There was an understandable fear that, if turned back to the British, they never would be recovered.

Another problem with British control of the Irish bases would be that it would bring back operating personnel in British military uniforms. This was unthinkable to most Irish citizens of all political persuasions.

On the other hand, control of the treaty ports and bases by the United States for the duration of hostilities would clearly be seen as a temporary measure. American uniformed men and women would probably be well received anywhere in Ireland. The improvement in air-field and port facilities made by the United States would be of lasting benefit to Ireland.

In order to be implemented, my plan must have the approval of the three parties: Ireland, Britain and the United States. I decided that no attempt should be made to seek the approval of either de Valera and the Irish government or that of President Roosevelt and the American government until the acquiescence of the British authorities was secured. The British had for years held the bases on a claim of sovereign right. When the Irish Free State was set up, they had secured continued British control of the bases in the terms of the treaty establishing the new dominion status. Just before the war started, they had returned control of them to Ireland but had since made various appeals to recover them.

Of the large number of people in many different walks of life that I met in Dublin and in other cities and towns of Ireland, only one man struck me as having appropriate qualifications for bringing to British authorities my proposal for lending the 'treaty ports' to the United States. That man was Emmet Dalton.

I was first introduced to Dalton by Norman Barfield, the young branch manager of Paramount Pictures for Ireland. In 1943, Dalton was nominally the supervisor of the Paramount film distributing branches in Northern Ireland, Scotland, Wales and Ireland. He made frequent trips to the film-distribution branch centres. I never knew whether he had or did not have intelligence duties in addition to his film distribution activities. So far as I was concerned, it made no difference one way or the other. Emmet Dalton had a distinguished record as a worker for a free and independent Ireland and had served in the British Army. While he was by no means unique in having a background in the British military, it was very unusual that such a young man had risen so rapidly in that service. He rose from recruit at the age of seventeen to major at his retirement and was awarded the Military Cross when he was only twenty-one.

In 1919, out of the army and back in Ireland, Dalton joined the IRA and soon became a trusted associate of Michael Collins. For a time he was the head of training for IRA forces. He led a brave but unsuccessful effort to free Sean MacEoin, Irish leader, from prison. After the treaty ending the Anglo-Irish War was approved by the Dáil – and de Valera and his associates walked out — Dalton was the Irish officer charged by Collins to clear the Four Courts Building of the anti-Treaty forces which had seized it. Using artillery borrowed from the stores left behind by the British when they turned over control to the Irish Free State, Dalton's men accomplished the mission, which was the first large-scale military action in the Civil War.

Dalton likewise was present in the action which had the unintended result of bringing about the end of the Civil War. This was the ambush of Collins by anti-Treaty men which resulted in his death at Bealnablath on 22 August 1922. At that time Dalton was a general in the Free State Army in charge of the Cork area. After the war he was Clerk of the Seanad Éireann.

The rumour I heard in Dublin in 1943 was that Dalton had been approached early in the war by the British High Command to head the British Commandos – a post made famous by Lord Louis Mountbatten. Being over forty years of age, however, according to the story, Dalton could not meet the medical and physical qualifications for commando-type operations.

My meetings with Dalton took place in the private back room of the Paramount film exchange, a room usually occupied by the branch manager except when the supervisor was in town. After I had got to know him and he was comfortable with me, I outlined in detail my proposal that the Irish bases be made available to the United States for the balance of the war. I knew the ultimate goal of Dalton and all the revolutionists, either pro-Treaty or anti-Treaty, was the same – the ending of Partition, making the whole island of Ireland again one country. United States help to end Partition would be critical.

Dalton agreed without hesitation to get the reaction of the appropriate British authorities to the plan. He did not tell me how he was going to proceed on his next trip to London, which was coming soon; all I knew was that he had maintained excellent contacts in the British government. That was all I needed at that point. He did not know I was with the OSS. He did know, however, that I had contacts in the film world who had excellent access to President Roosevelt.

Following an indication of approval or at least acqui-escence by the British, I hoped to present my plan to President Roosevelt through the good offices of William J. Donovan, the head of the OSS. Donovan was an American hero of World War I. As Colonel of New York's 'Fighting Irish' Sixty-ninth Regiment, he was awarded the United States' highest military honor, the Congressional Medal of Honor.

Although a prominent member of the Republican Party – he had been campaign manager for Herbert Hoover and a Republican candidate for Governor of New York State – General Donovan had ready access to the White House. President Roosevelt had made him a trusted adviser several years before the nation was at war. As a private citizen, Donovan did fact-finding for Roosevelt in Europe. In July 1941 – five months before the Japanese attack on Pearl Harbour – the President made him head of the newly created agency in the Executive Office of the President, the Coordinator of Information. On 13 June 1942, a part of that agency was transferred to the new OSS of the US Joint Chiefs of Staff. Donovan, called back into military service, was made director of the new agency.

Donovan knew me, knew my OSS work in Ireland and was a friend of my father.

Roosevelt was not known to have special sympathy for the Irish or for Catholics generally – he came out of the old American Protestant tradition – but he was extremely sensitive to political issues and the current voting strength of Irish-Americans. Two of his principal political associates were Catholic: James Farley, his former campaign manager, and Frank Walker, the Postmaster General. The Irish voting strength in the United States, concentrated in the major cities of the North, was critical in the election of a Democrat to the White House.

Roosevelt would also be attracted by the military aspects

of a loan of the Irish bases, particularly Cobh. As a yachtsman and former Secretary of the Navy, he had a particular interest in issues affecting the navy. Access to Cobh would be something the Navy Department would like to have.

Finally, the idea of a reunification of Ireland would appeal to FDR. Americans have an aversion to colonialism but firm respect for 'states' rights.' The elimination of Partition would justly and inevitably result in a great deal of autonomy for four of the Irish Provinces, with the central government in Dublin mostly involved with matters such as currency, trade and foreign relations.

Once Roosevelt's endorsement of the deal had been obtained and the British had agreed to it or at least were in a permissive posture, I was prepared to seek de Valera's cooperation. I was optimistic that his approval could be obtained but realistic about the difficulties involved.

De Valera had spent years articulating his vision of neutrality, together with his repeated refusal to permit under any circumstances the return of the Treaty-port facilities to the British. Yet the proposition that the bases be lent to the United States was clearly a different proposition than returning them to Britain. There would be no possibility of America wanting to retain the Irish bases indefinitely. It would be hard for either the British or Irish government to resist pressures from the American government backed up by the very strong influence of Irish-Americans. It is not too much to say that there would have been no successful Irish war against the British and no Irish Free State and hence no Ireland without the financial and moral support that came to the Irish revolutionaries from the US.

The prime argument for persuading de Valera, however,

was the assurance that the United States would exert 'best interest' in ending Partition. Here was a realistic chance of attaining the long-sought goal of a united Ireland, a goal shared by all political parties in Ireland. It was foreseen that at the end of the war the United States would be the most powerful country in the world. Britain would not be able to resist strong pressures from Washington to end Partition: it would be looking to the United States for all kinds of assistance to help it recover from the long years of the war, including the great physical destruction caused by bombings. After all, Partition had been in effect for less than a quarter of a century.

Surely there would be opposition to a united Ireland among many in the North who had prospered politically and economically since Partition and there would be fears of domination by Dublin. Unlike previously, however, pro-Partition advocates would not be able to employ effective military force. Northern Ireland was by now a military camp for US troops. From both the practical and the psychological point of view, violence by those who wished to maintain a union of the six counties of Northern Ireland with the United Kingdom would not be a tenable option.

Guarantees of religious and political rights of all in the North by the United States would do much to soothe the emotional trauma of an end to Partition. Some unhappiness was bound to be felt in the North by the end of Partition, but time is a great healer. Reasonable people on both sides of the Atlantic, and in both the North and South of Ireland, would quite quickly get used to the idea of one Ireland with a special relationship to both Britain and the United States.

I awaited further word from Dalton with keen anticipation. When he let me know the result of his inquiry, though, I had no reason to rejoice.

Dalton's report was that the British Imperial General Staff was quite content with the existing situation with regard to the treaty ports and wanted nothing done to change the situation. The word was, 'Leave things as they are.'

In the eyes of the British High Command – as I understood it from Dalton's comments to me – the Allies had by now, in mid-1943, all the military bases they needed. Additional bases would require outfitting and new defences, personnel would be diverted and, perhaps most importantly, operation of bases in Ireland by the US would open the door to much heavier bombing by German aircraft. That would require a diversion of anti-aircraft guns and other facilities to be spread throughout the twenty-six counties because the Germans would classify Ireland as a belligerent.

I never knew whether the post-war quid pro quo that would bring US pressure for the end of Partition was a factor considered by the British Imperial General Staff before the response to Dalton. This, of course, is a possibility. Although the record may never be clear, the potential opportunity for an early end of Partition was lost.

Taoiseach Éamon de Valera, whom Quigley met in 1943
(photo: Colman Doyle)

Frank Aiken, Minister for the Coordination of Defensive Measures during World War II

(photo: Colman Doyle)

Sean T. O'Kelly, Tánaiste and Minister for Finance during World War II

(photo: Colman Doyle)

Emmet Dalton, whom Quigley used to sound out the British on his plan for Ireland to lend the 'treaty ports' to Britain, here photographed with Michael Collins at Portobello Barracks in 1922

(photo: Meda Ryan)

Louis Elliman, who ran film theatres, a film-distribution company and a stage theatre in Ireland (on far right) with, from left, scriptwriter Harry O'Donovan, William Boyd (Hopalong Cassidy) and actor Jimmy O'Dea

(photo: *Evening Herald*)

R. Carter Nicholas, Desk Officer, Irish Desk, OSS, Washington, DC
(photo: Robert C. Nicholas)

OSS Director William J. Donovan
(photo: *Motion Picture Herald*)

Will H. Hays, President of Motion Picture Producers & Distributors of America, who provided Quigley's commercial cover

(photo: *Motion Picture Herald*)

Governor Carl E. Milliken, Foreign Manager of Motion Picture Producers & Distributors of America, who passed Quigley's reports to OSS headquarters

(photo: *Motion Picture Herald*)

Francis P. Miller, head of British Empire, Afghanistan and Ireland
Section, OSS Strategic Intelligence, 1942–3
(photo: Francis Pickens Miller Papers (#9760), Special Collections
Department, University of Virginia Library)

W. H. Shepardson, head of OSS Strategic Intelligence
(photo: John Shepardson)

5

There's a Neutrality On

During World War II the most important and, to many outsiders, the strangest action of the Irish was their neutrality.

Officially, out of the thirty-two countries of the whole island, the twenty-six which form an independent nation – linked externally with the British Commonwealth of Nations – were neutral. Northern Ireland, as an integral part of the United Kingdom, entered the war on 3 September 1939. In fact, Ireland was a non-belligerent and not a real neutral, although the Irish government had dismayed people on both sides of the Atlantic by appearing at times to be 'leaning over backwards' in its efforts to be completely neutral.

Like many other peoples, the Irish, as a nation, do not like war. More than a number of other nations, they have seen much fighting at close hand. Ireland had experienced a revolution in 1916, several years of guerrilla struggle against the British and a civil war. The conditions there were similar to what would have resulted in the United States had the Revolutionary War been followed immediately by the Civil War and then only two decades of peace. The Irishmen who were in leadership positions – as well as almost all of the adults – had seen a great deal of war and the effects of armed strife.

As the war clouds gathered in Europe, Ireland had tried to remain uninvolved in the conflict, if possible. The official policy of neutrality was proclaimed long before the outbreak of the war and was endorsed by virtually the entire population.

Although the British government considered it to be part of the British Commonwealth of Nations, Ireland had a legal right to choose what stand it wished with regard to a war. The Statute of Westminster of 1931 fully acknowledged the right of the Dominions to enter or stay aloof from any war in which England is engaged.

In February 1939, the following statement was made in an official broadcast over Radio Éireann: 'The desire of the Irish people and the desire of the Irish government is to keep our nation out of war. The aim of government policy is to maintain and preserve our neutrality in the event of war.'

In a private interview in August 1939, de Valera said, 'Ireland wants to be neutral and no one loves a neutral. The neutrality policy which Éire had adopted was pleasing to no nation, for none of the powerful European countries liked a neutral because the smaller nations were expected to line up on the side of one of the major powers.'

At the time of the Nazi invasion of Poland, which started on 1 September 1939, de Valera reemphasised Ireland's neutrality.

Although officially neutral, Éire supplied a great deal in manpower to the cause of the United Nations against the Axis powers and provided an enormous amount of agricultural products. Its contribution was as follows:

1   Manpower. Precise figures are not available but it seems certain that about 150,000 Irish citizens volunteered for the British Army and the Royal Air Force. Since volunteers had to cross the Irish Sea, they signed up in English or Welsh cities. There was no practical way to distinguish between the citizens of Ireland and, say, the 'Liverpool Irish' and other Irish men and women living in Britain. An equal or even greater number of Irish went to England to work in war plants or in vital agricultural pursuits. This manpower contribution takes on further significance when it is realised that the entire population of Ireland was less than 3 million.

2   Agricultural produce. Cattle, bacon, milk, cheese, tinned meats and certain vegetables needed in Britain went by sea in a continuous flow throughout the war.

3   Military protection. A neutral or non-belligerent Ireland provided a certain amount of protection for England's flank. That does not mean Ireland helped to prevent an invasion, because the country would probably have been invaded at the same time as any move against England. However, under the neutrality emergency the Irish called into service all their military reserves and enrolled thousands for duration enlistments. Also, if Ireland were a belligerent, munitions and supplies, especially anti-aircraft equipment and fighter planes, would have had to be diverted from other sectors.

4   Civil peace. For the first time in many wars, there were no internal difficulties and strife for Britain to contend with in Ireland. Those who served abroad

went voluntarily. The military forces at home in Ireland realised that they were serving their own country first and, depending on the individual, understood that they were also serving the general cause.

5 Absence of ruin. If Ireland were vigorously attacked from the air by the Nazis, England would have the additional problem of providing food and relief. England had enough problems of that kind without the burden of taking care of thousands of Irishmen, many of whom would have been in a desperate plight. Ireland was seriously exposed to air attack, being without proper fighter or anti-aircraft defences. Its towns and cities had great slum areas, where enemy bombers might have brought frightful havoc. Furthermore, the transportation system of Ireland has never been adequate: a few bombs would have crippled it. Appeals for food and other relief items would have resulted. These would have had to come from America or from England's small supply. In either case, England would have been the loser.

Other, less important points show that Ireland was not strictly speaking a neutral in World War II. The country had a complete financial union with England and received most of its imports through that country. The Irish government accepted the English pound as equivalent to the Irish punt. As a result, Éire had been building up balances in the Bank of England. Most of what England obtained in Éire during the war cost simply the price of printing and the paper for the necessary pound notes.

The Nazi government evidently was under no illusions about Ireland's position. Some of the best ships in Ireland's small merchant marine were sunk by German submarines in broad daylight. Planes attacked Irish ships, and German bombs were dropped on the mainland of Ireland.

The Irish realised that proclaimed neutrality had never been a protection from the Nazis for any small nation. They knew that many of the countries Germany had invaded in the early years of the war were neutral or even had treaties of alliance with her. The Irish knew that the Nazi military had drawn up plans for an invasion of Ireland; this was likely to be attempted as a flanking action at the same time as – or a short time before – an attempted invasion of England.

Despite the realities of the situation, the Irish government assiduously cultivated the idea of neutrality, perhaps to keep its people as calm as possible during the Emergency.

Ireland's neutrality was genuine in some respects. It allowed the Germans to maintain their legation and the Japanese their consulate. During the first years of the war, when the Nazi war machine was overrunning most of the European Continent, the small staff of the German legation made itself conspicuous with the press and in some other Irish quarters. Later, they became less obtrusive. The few Japanese consular officials became social outcasts after Pearl Harbour.

While some Irishmen, chiefly on account of deep-rooted feelings against the British, were pro-German, one could not discover a single Irishman who might have been termed pro-Japanese in any sense. Further, the number of pro-Germans was probably never over a few thousand, and this group dwindled as the character of the Nazi system became increasingly clear to the Irish.

Officially, the Irish government may have engaged in more diplomatic tightrope-walking than was either necessary or expedient. De Valera, of course, directed Irish foreign affairs. Joseph Walshe, as Secretary for External Affairs, was entrusted with carrying out much of the policy. The Irish people would probably have supported the expulsion of the German Minister and his staff on 1 September 1939, the day of the Nazi invasion of Poland. Such a severance of diplomatic relations between Ireland and Germany would not have had to result in war, and Ireland could have continued with its non-belligerent policy. The Catholics of Ireland, who had a predominant influence in th country in many ways, would be expected to have approved such a vigorous protest against the destruction of Catholic Poland.

The typical Irishman would have preferred to see the German legation and the Japanese consulate closed throughout the war. There was particular objection to the Japanese, who had not been represented in Ireland before the war. Aversion on the part of the Irish to the Japanese Consul General and Consul undoubtedly crippled the activities of these bodies.

In March 1944, the Irish government rejected the request made by the US government that the Axis diplomatic representatives be expelled to prevent espionage activities affecting the safety of American and other Allied forces preparing to invade the Continent. The British and other Commonwealth governments supported the American position. The American government naturally wished to take all possible steps to avoid jeopardizing the lives of members of the Allied armed forces; the Irish government asserted its undeniable right under international law to remain neutral.

David Gray, the American Minister, together with members of his small staff, did what he could to make the Irish leaders understand the US position.

To develop and carry on certain aspects of its neutrality, the Irish government made sweeping use of censorship. One effect of this policy was a passion for anonymity among newspaper, magazine, and other writers. Articles appeared under every kind of pseudonym or signature. Also, in certain quarters there was fear of getting into trouble through the spoken word.

In the midst of the Emergency it was natural that the government should impose some kind of censorship. In the American view, press censorship should be kept to the absolute minimum. In peace there should be none; in war the only information that should be withheld is that which is of direct military aid to the enemy. In Ireland, the censorship went so far beyond military or even political necessity that its true purpose is difficult to see.

Some Irishmen believe that the Irish government tried to use the powers of emergency censorship to control thought. The political parties agreed at the start of the Emergency that censorship of opinion was needed as an aid against internal strife. Although there was no agreement that the news should be censored, censorship of the news took place.

In endeavoring to uphold strict neutrality the Irish government during the war fell into most unreasonable varieties of censorship. For example, in September 1943, for the first time in Irish history, the government film censorship authority decided that the American flag should be cut from a motion picture. Except for the green, white and orange of the Irish flag, the American flag is held in highest esteem among the Irish. Censoring the American flag in Ireland is a strange act: Ireland owes a great deal to the United States, and virtually every family in Ireland has extremely close ties with America.

Of a multitude of trivial acts of censorship, the following, selected at random, may be cited: the newspapers could not list the British Broadcasting Programs under the heads 'Home Service and Armed Service'! They were required to say merely 'Home Service and Alternative Service.' Newspapers could not mention the connection of any Irish man or woman with the British forces. A reference to Kaiser, the American shipbuilder, was cut from a film because it was asserted that some in the cinema audiences might think it meant Kaiser Wilhelm of World War I.

Editors tried to get around the censorship as best they could. Some of the tricks used were ingenious but little was accomplished. The government crackdown was swift and hard.

The censorship even censored itself; that is, newspapermen and other writers were forbidden under penalty of law to disclose the fact of censorship. They were not allowed to say that the censor took such and such action. Not even in returning an article to a contributor could they tell him that the censor declined to approve it. There could have been an excuse for the censorship if the Irish people had not known 'there was a neutrality on' (as some put it), but the Irish people knew what was happening. Most families had a member in the British armed forces or in war factories. All had friends who suffered from battle and the blitz. Also the BBC news and British newspapers were heard and read almost everywhere in Ireland.

Apart from the neutrality-dictated press and film censor-ship, there was set in motion a censorship of books which, in its way, seems to be the most extreme. Even medical books have been censored. It is said that every Irish writer of note has been 'honoured' by having at least one of his works banned in his own country. On the other hand, Donald J. Giltinan, who worked in the government's postal censorship, wrote and had produced in one of Dublin's leading theaters during the summer of 1943 an original play, *This Book Is Banned*, a comedy on censorship.

All the wartime censorship was controlled by Frank Aiken, Minister for the Coordination of Defensive Measures (in effect, Minister for Censorship). Aiken was Chief of Staff of the IRA when de Valera gave up the civil war against the Irish Free State. The postal and press censors and Richard Hayes, the film censor, were all subject to Aiken's censorship orders. Even high-ranking government officials, including Sean T. O'Kelly, the Tánaiste (vice-Taoiseach) and Minister for Finance, chafed under Aiken's censorship of their addresses.

Freedom of the press and of expression generally, as known in the United States, did not exist in Ireland while there was 'a neutrality on.'

The use of the term 'neutral' as applied to the twenty-six counties of Ireland was a misnomer. Irish neutrality was a myth cultivated for long-term political reasons by de Valera and his government and encouraged, again for long-term political reasons, by Winston Churchill and his government. The matter was further complicated by the fact that the two men disliked one another.

The correct definition of Ireland's status in World War

II was that of a non-belligerent. Neutrality implies that the country gives no moral support to either side and trades on equal footing with the belligerents. During the war Ireland had no trade with Germany or Italy and sought none and was certainly was not a trading partner of Japan.

In the early years of the war, some people in Ireland, including a few in high places, would have liked the country to be a real neutral and not merely a neutral by myth. This was for reasons other than admiration of Nazism. In addition, only a relative handful of Irishmen admired Mussolini for the fascist orderliness typified by Italian trains running on time. Basic to such opinion was a fear that Hitler's forces would defeat Britain as they had defeated almost all of Europe. If Nazism had triumphed and Hitler had his boastful wish of dictating the peace for a thousand years, some in Ireland thought they would fare better should they be able to plead their country's neutrality in the crisis.

That was an absurd dream for two reasons. Firstly, Hitler had repeatedly shown that he did not respect the rights of any nation. Secondly, both he and the decision-makers in the German government were well aware that Ireland was neither a neutral or a non-belligerent.

Ireland, as a small country, had to take the way in which the Nazi war machine had treated other European countries as a warning. The persecution by the Nazis of Jews, Poles and others was not unknown in Ireland.

Even before the Japanese went to war with the United States, the citizens and government of Ireland were providing great assistance to Britain. The contribution of the women and men of the twenty-six counties of Ireland to the eventual defeat of the Nazis and their allies was enormous. This service was given in both the armed forces of Britain and the factories which turned out war material. Furthermore, Ireland was an agricultural resource of great significance to Britain. None of its food exports during the war went to Germany or to Continental ports, where it could be made available to the Nazis.

Basic to this situation were financial links. Ireland at the time had a financial union of linked currencies with Britain. Food and other imports during the war were paid for by Britain with paper money. As a result, in its relatively small way the Irish government and the country's people bore part of the cost of the war effort.

Sympathy with the Japanese was non-existent. Ireland and its citizens became even less neutral and more non-belligerent after the war in the Pacific commenced. Anti-British feeling has existed in Ireland for centuries, but the United States from its founding has enjoyed only the best of feelings.

From the time America entered the war the Irish government took increasing steps to be helpful to the Allied pursuit of victory. Much of that cooperation was kept secret for what must be considered political reasons. High Irish government officials and military officers maintained liaison with the OSS through regular visits to Dublin from the OSS offices in London and in Washington. There was full cooperation with OSS X-2 (Counter-Intelligence) Branch. Communications of Irish diplomats stationed abroad were made available to the American government.

From the beginning of the war German aviators who landed in Ireland were interned. Allied fighters of whatever nationality who landed on Irish soil were deemed to have been on training missions and were returned to their bases. A number of rescued German sailors were also interned for the duration of the war.

Throughout the war, cable service from Dublin to the Continent, which was available to the German diplomats, went through England, where the messages were deciphered. In return, the Germans allowed the cable link from Switzerland to England to remain open. The German diplomats in Ireland were not allowed to use their radio transmitter. As an extra precaution, Irish authorities removed the radio transmitter from the German Legation some months prior to the Allied invasion of Normandy.

6

BACK AT OSS HEADQUARTERS

I reported to no one in Ireland. No one there saw my reports, which reached my superiors in Washington, DC, usually by a circuitous route. One set of the most important documents was, however, hand-delivered to the OSS office in London and another set was taken personally to the Que Building, the headquarters of the OSS's secret-intelligence division.

Que Building was a large, low, temporary structure at the end of Constitution Avenue, a short distance across parkland from the Lincoln Memorial overlooking the Potomac River. The OSS also occupied space taken over from the US National Public Health Service, which was at the top of a hill overlooking Que Building. OSS Director William J. Donovan had his office in the old public-health building.

In November 1942 I was assigned to the British Empire, Afghanistan and Ireland section of the strategic-intelligence division, which was headed by Francis Peckins Miller, a lawyer from Virginia. When I first met Miller, his administrative assistant, Tom Beale, asked, 'Who is going to be in charge of Quigley?' Miller replied, 'We are.'

The section which Miller headed, with its curious

juxtaposition of Afghanistan and Ireland (these countries were dealt with together because they both had a relationship with the British Empire), was a fairly small part of Whitney Shepardson's strategic-intelligence division. Miller and Shepardson had been friends and colleagues since the Treaty of Versailles negotiations after World War I.

As Donovan built up his organisations he turned to his friends and to friends of friends: with a long background in the law and politics, he had very extensive personal connections. Although he was a Republican – he had run unsuccessfully for Governor of New York and had been Herbert Hoover's campaign manager during Hoover's successful presidential bid – Donovan had developed warm relations with FDR. The value of the informational insights provided by Donovan to the president over several years motivated him to make Donovan head of the United States' first comprehensive foreign-intelligence agency.

The mission of the OSS, as a wartime agency, was to help win the war as swiftly as possible. The OSS was an arm of the US Joint Chiefs of Staff. Donovan was never out of his army uniform, which, until the Japanese surrendered, was often adorned with the ribbon of the Congressional Medal of Honour for his heroism in World War I.

The activities of Donovan's agency were carried out in four divisions: intelligence (SI); special operations (SO), which carried out commando-type combat operations; research and analysis (R&A), which was staffed primarily with academics, and X-2, which handled counter-intelligence – the seeking out of enemy agents. Much of the work of the R&A division was carried out at the Washington headquarters. The work of the other three divisions was done mostly in the field, with recruitment, training and supervision directed by Washington.

One evening while I was training in December 1942 at a secret location in the Maryland countryside, Tom Beale brought me to meet R. Carter Nicholas, who had just joined the OSS. Nicholas had been called up for active duty prior to Pearl Harbour as a reserve naval officer but for health reasons had been returned to civilian status. Like so many in the OSS, he had a broad range of friendships dating from college and many family connections. He was a member of the 'poor' branch of the family of the founder of a small surgical-bandage company which became the international pharmaceutical company Johnson & Johnson. From then on throughout the war, Carter Nicholas served as the OSS's Irish-desk officer. He was my immediate superior. When, in mid-1943, Francis Miller was commissioned in the army and transferred to the French section, Nicholas reported directly to the SI division head, Whitney Shepardson, and also on occasion to Donovan.

My two lengthy special reports (neither of which has been declassified by the US government, more than half a century later) were passed directly to Donovan. I wrote the first of these reports in London in August 1943; I wrote the second in New York and hand-delivered it to Nicholas at a secret location in Washington away from the US government facility.

My regular or routine reports (which are reproduced in the latter part of this book) were processed in the OSS's Washington headquarters by Nicholas as they arrived on his desk. His editing was sensitive to the need to preserve my commercial cover as a representative of the American film industry. Even in dissemination of my reports within the OSS organisation, for example to the R&A division, Nicholas tried to make sure that the fact that I was an OSS agent would go unnoticed.

Material in both my regular reports and the two special reports were used by Nicholas in two other ways: they were a prime source of names for the 'watch list' of name files which Nicholas and his assistant built up on over 1,000 people in Ireland and the United States. Included on that list, surprisingly, was David Gray, American Minister to Ireland, due to the identity of some of his contacts.

The second personal use Nicholas made of my reports – and the most important for him – was in personal conversations on Irish issues, especially neutrality, he had with officials at the US State Department and with military officials.

The next section of this book consists of the actual reports sent by me to the Irish Desk in the Strategic Intelligence Branch of the OSS at headquarters in Washington. They were declassified and made available to me at the United States National Archives, College Park, Maryland in May 1997, fifty-four years after they were written in Dublin and London. Some others of my Irish OSS reports have either been lost or, for unimaginable reasons, are still being kept secret by the US government.

PART II

TEXT OF OSS REPORTS

London, 24 May 1943

Dear Governor

As I advised you by cable on May 22 I was delayed here in London by a visa technicality. While I was on the way over, the Irish authorities issued a new visa regulation. It so happened that I was the first to submit a visa issued in New York following the passage of the new regulation. A technical point was involved as to whether my unexpired New York visa was still good or whether a new one would have to be issued to me here in London. I expected an answer first last Monday afternoon, May 17. No word came and I communicated with Walter McNally, an RKO manager and theatre operator in Dublin whom I know, and the matter was settled immediately – the New York visa was ruled satisfactory.

The British Passport Office, of course, could not issue me with an exit permit until the matter of the Irish visa had been decided. I have been informed by telephone that the permit is ready and I will pick it up today. Last Monday the British office also had me call at the passport section of the American Embassy to make sure that my passport was properly validated for Éire. As expected, it was in order. The point arose because evidently the State Department in Washington stamps 'Ireland' on a passport when both parts of the country are included whereas the British authorities use 'Éire' at all times to refer to the part which used to be called the Irish Free State.

While in London I have had an opportunity to call on the managing directors of the American group of film companies here. They have all been very cooperative and at the suggestion of Mr Allport have written to their managers in Dublin informing them of my visit. From the American managing directors I learned that the motion picture problem in Éire is probably now even worse than it has been in recent months. A short time ago the companies had to stop making a special newsreel for there and since the regular newsreel issues are generally not passed by the Irish Film Censor authorities it is reported that virtually no newsreel is now circulated. Also a considerable number of war films are now arriving from America and these are regularly turned down by the censors. This has resulted in a continually diminishing quantity of new films being available for that country.

I intend to leave for Dublin early tomorrow morning. I plan to stay at one of the larger hotels for a time, during which I can find a suitable place, probably at one of the smaller hotels. By the time you receive this I will have cabled you my address.

Today is the first day in which we have had any rain since I arrived. The weather has been surprisingly good.

The Shelbourne Hotel, Dublin, Éire, 29 May 1943
Dear Governor
Walter McNally, RKO Radio Pictures distributor and

operator of several theatres and cafés, met me at the boat on Tuesday evening. He had reserved a room for me at the Shelbourne. That was fortunate, for it is extremely difficult to get a hotel room in this city. There are many visitors.

This week I have seen several of the film company branch managers and probably next Wednesday I shall have an informal meeting with all of them.

On Thursday I had lunch with Dr Hayes, the film censor, and then spent some time with him in his office. He was very cooperative. He invited me to attend his next screening of a feature film on which cuts may be expected so I can see just what action he takes.

As you know I was given a letter of introduction to Mr Gray, the American Minister, by Frank Walker. I phoned the legation on Thursday afternoon and asked to speak to the Minister's office and the first thing I knew I was surprised to find that the voice on the other end of the line identified himself as Mr Gray. Next, I was surprised by his invitation to lunch the following day.

There was an interesting and diverse gathering at the small luncheon at the Legation presided over by Mr and Mrs Gray. Guests were the Apostolic Delegate and his secretary, Richard Watts, who is going to Chungking shortly, a man from Mr Watts's office in London and two rather elderly Irish gentlemen. Mr Gray sat me next to him and during lunch expressed great interest in motion pictures and the particular problems affecting films here. He said that he would have liked to present me to de Valera but he is leaving for America next week. I told him that I had letters of introduction to de Valera from the Archbishop of Los Angeles and Martin Conboy. Gray told me to write a note to de Valera enclosing the letters and requesting an appointment. He added that when he saw de Valera that afternoon he would mention that I was here for the Motion Picture Producers and Distributors in connection with film censorship and other related questions.

Yesterday afternoon I had a meeting with the three branch managers who handle – or rather, used to handle – newsreels here. Following that meeting and other conversations I cabled suggesting that a few prints of the United newsreel made up in the United States for such countries as Portugal, Sweden, Switzerland and Turkey be sent here by plane for censorship-test purposes.

2 June 1943
Dear Governor

Last Saturday I sent to de Valera my letters of introduction from Archbishop Cantwell and Martin Conboy together with a brief note saying that I would deeply appreciate the privilege of an appointment at his convenience. On Monday I received word that de Valera would see me on Tuesday afternoon. It was a particular favor to be able to see him at this time because today, Wednesday, he started his election tour of the country, which, I believe, may keep him away until after the election on June 22.

As I mentioned to you I was introduced to de Valera, or an Taoiseach, which is his official title, when my father met him at the time of the Horse Show here in the summer of 1939. Now, as then, a large reproduction of the Lincoln Memorial statue of Lincoln and framed reproductions of the Declaration of Independence dominate the reception room next to his office.

I realised how busy de Valera was, especially with the election campaign on, and intended to stay only a few moments, but his remarks on the motion picture were so interesting that before I realised it I had been in his office for half an hour. De Valera, as you probably know, is charming to meet and, like the present Pope, is a much better-looking man than photographs would lead you to expect.

He first remarked about the pile of papers on his desk, saying that he was going to be away from the city and would have to take with him all the papers he might need as there would not be anywhere where any statistics he wanted could be looked up. The secretary came in to ask about a particular tentative speaking date, and de Valera then said to me that he would not speak at any fair for there people would be more interested in the cattle and other attractions and would not wish to listen to any speech.

De Valera said that he believed that the motion picture was the most potent force for instruction in the world: he said he thought it was much more powerful than the press or books because it demanded so much less of its audience. As an example he said that he was now reading a book of Jack London as translated into the Irish. While he could enjoy the book and represent in his mind the Arctic lands in the story he noted that some people would not take the trouble to read a book and could gain knowledge through the cinema. At this point he said that he strongly objected to faking in motion-picture scenes.

The motion picture, de Valera hopes, will play its part in one of the two ends announced in the campaign – i.e. in the drive for greater use of the Irish language. (The other main end is the abolition of Partition.)

De Valera said that after the election he proposes to open a drive to increase the spoken use of Irish. This he plans to do whether reelected or not, though of course he noted that he would probably have more influence in this regard if he were elected. He said that he thought a phrase in Irish could be thrown on the screen before each motion-picture show. Perhaps a proverb or similar expression would be used. The idea was that people in the audience who knew Irish would translate the words for their neighbors, whose curiosity would be aroused.

De Valera wants the films to elevate and educate. He made no comment about the great use of motion pictures for mere amusement and entertainment. As an example he said that he had instructed the people running the Irish Radio Station to produce programs which would elevate the tastes of the audience. This is done even though, as he remarked, people who do not wish to listen to such a program twist the dials and tune in to another station. (This, I assume, would mean either the BBC regular program or the special program put on chiefly for the forces. Other stations are also tuned in. A waiter told us the other day that he had been listening in to Radio Tokyo.)

In explaining briefly the purpose of my visit I mentioned that all Irish matters, including films, have a potential public relations aspect in the United States. De Valera said he hopes for closer links with America in the future and indicated that a goal of Irish policy was to be a bridge between Europe and America in the post-war world.

I told de Valera that I had cabled New York to find out whether you and the film companies might be able to arrange to send a few prints of newsreels made up there for such other neutral countries as Portugal, Sweden, Switzerland and

Turkey for submission, as a test, to the film censor.

De Valera expressed the hope that in the future Éire may have a small film industry to produce educational pictures. He said that he had at first thought that the climate of this country was not suitable for film production as it is not suitable for astronomical work but later he decided that since much of modern production is done in indoor studios it would be possible to make pictures here. He said that a report had been prepared on the general subject but I gathered from his manner of speaking that plans for action in this regard had been put off into the future, probably to the end of the war.

I asked de Valera about the censoring of the film *The Eternal Gift,* which is merely the Catholic High Mass produced by the Servite Fathers in Chicago and bearing the endorsement of the Archbishop of Chicago and a commentary by Monsignor Fulton J. Sheen of the Catholic University. It was rejected both for public and private exhibition about a year ago. De Valera said that he would take the same position so far as public exhibition was concerned as this country is so Catholic that representation of a Catholic religious service, no matter how treated, would be objectionable. He said he did not know the reasons in connection with the ban on private exhibition and suggested that I ask Dr Hayes, the film censor. I shall do this, for Dr Hayes has been most pleasant and cooperative.

Before leaving I said that I hoped that I would be able to see him again when he would not be so busy and de Valera said that I should call up his secretary for an appointment when I wished. At the door of his office, de Valera asked whether I had met his brother, a priest in the United States, but I have not. As I was walking down the stairs out of the government Buildings I could not help but recall the contrast between my impression of de Valera in 1939 and now: in 1939 he appeared to me to be a very tired and possibly somewhat discouraged man; today he seemed in perfect health and looking ahead with pleasure to the speaking tour around the country and the tasks which he plans to undertake with renewed vigor in the future.

4 July 1943
Dear Governor

This will cover the period from June 28 to July 3.

On Monday Dr Hayes, the film censor, took me to lunch. Although I have been seeing him several times a week at his office it was also pleasant to have a chat over lunch. As I have mentioned previously he is a careful, conscientious, scholarly man who has a rather trying job these days. A censor can never please everyone. Dr Hayes however is really charming and has a good sense of humor. He has told me some interesting and amusing stories. Like many other men in public life or public office in this country he was imprisoned by the British during the 'troubles.' For many years he has been a close personal friend of important members of the government.

Dr Hayes is taking his annual vacation now and will be away from his office during the whole of July. He expects to be out of town for a fortnight and after that would be available, if necessary, to advise the acting censor, Michael J. Dolan, the Abbey actor who is currently appearing in one of the plays as well as looking after his job as deputy censor for films. In order not to cause Dolan any possible embarrassment during his first week 'on his own' I plan to be away for a week. As you wish, I am going to visit some of the cities and towns. At first I thought that I would take a swing around the island lasting two or three weeks. Then I decided to break it up so as not to be away from Dublin more than about a week at a time. Another reason I have for going now for the first week trip is that during the middle of the month I hope to see some of the government officials whom I have not got in touch with previously on account of the election and the organisation of the new Dáil and government.

I plan to visit Galway, Limerick and Tralee (where a couple of old subscribers to *Motion Picture Herald* live) this week. I may also include Killarney, where Tom Cooper, who made the most recent Irish feature film, resides. At the end of the month I hope to visit the cities on the east coast, Waterford and Galway.

Fair progress evidently is being made in connection with my work here. It is hard to be sure because each motion picture has its own problem. Figures on films passed, rejected and cut do not necessarily show a great deal because in each particular month different pictures come up for censorship. It may just happen that this week no picture may cause serious question and next week a large number may be rejected entirely. The first picture to be rejected entirely during the month I have been here was turned down last week. It is *They Have Got Me Covered*, a Bob Hope comedy which concerns spies, etc., in Washington. A comedy really should not be taken too seriously. On the other hand, *Flight for Freedom* (RKO) and *Aerial Gunner* (Paramount) recently came through with relatively minor cuts. Now when looking at a film with the censor I can tell in about three-quarters of the cases what he will cut but I am frequently surprised very much by the other quarter.

This week there came to my notice an item in the British trade paper *Today's Cinema* (June 22 issue) which evidently was based on opinion supplied directly or indirectly by someone at the London office of one of the American film companies. The item read:

'Hints I've had from one or two quarters lead me to believe that Martin Quigley Jr's mission to Ireland hasn't been unfruitful. Quigley arrived in England a month or so back, bent on journeying to the Emerald Isle as emissary of the MPPDA and discussing there the thorny question of providing films suitable for Éire.

'Whether the results of his contact will be made known soon, or whether they'll be made public at all, is something I can't say. But the feeling I'm left with is that he's made a very good impression, and that there's every reason to hope difficulties will be less apparent in future.

'Which is something to make good hearing for exhibitors in Éire. They have been on very short commons for films for some time.'

That item, I am afraid, is far too much on the optimistic side. However, I believe at least the film censor here perhaps now has a somewhat better idea of the American motion picture industry's viewpoint on a number of matters; and I, on the other hand, have learned a number of interesting things about motion pictures in this country. I hope to report on these things to you when they become more clearly defined in my own mind.

In passing, let me tell you that Dr Hayes expressed a

comment to me that was rather pleasing – he pointed out that while he had no special fondness for Hollywood film product he found certain of the British films awful in comparison. The occasion for the remark was the screening of a poor English subject which contained a few scenes which would not be permitted on moral grounds under the American motion picture production code. I wish it were better known here that, from a moral point of view, the American motion picture is quite unobjectionable. The usual cuts are rather few on moral grounds and these involve applications and not principles. Certain dances are cut here, as well as some remarks.

I do regret, however, that because so many films are rejected under the Emergency Powers Order that the people and the educational and religious leaders here are currently getting a rather distorted view of the American motion picture. Now, roughly a third of the better American pictures are not being shown here or are so seriously cut that their entertainment quality is impaired. Recently I have been gathering some data on this subject running back about a year; not all the information is in yet but I can tell you that over thirty American feature films have been rejected by the war censorship and at least a dozen others have not been submitted by the companies because rejection was deemed certain. In addition, half a dozen or more short subjects have been rejected and an equal number not imported. Of course this does not include the pictures cut to a greater or lesser degree. Hardly a film goes by in which there is not at least one or more cuts under the Emergency War Powers Orders. Sometimes the cuts are simple to handle; in other cases the whole story of the picture may be ruined.

My contacts with the branch managers of the companies which distribute American films are regular. Hardly a day goes by that I do not see or speak to one or more of them about a particular film or talk about the general film situation. This past week I saw almost all of the managers.

I am now getting a chance to meet some of the exhibitors. They are much closer to the public than the branch managers and have good ideas on the reaction to various types of American films. This week I met Charles Jones, manager of the Grafton Theatre, which used to be one of the most important film theatres and is now a second-run place. J. M. Stanley of Drogheda had me up there on Saturday for a game of golf (my first since Pinehurst). Stanley operates three theatres in the Boyne area and also publishes the weekly *Argus*. We went out to the golf course (Baltray the most sporting I have ever seen) by jaunting car, and Stanley pointed out the local sites on the way. Drogheda is an old town and has a rather mixed population, including some Dutch and Belgians. It is, however, a prosperous place and a good motion-picture place. One or two more motion-picture theatres are to be constructed there in the near future. The southern part of the town is on one side of the Boyne in County Meath and the other part is in County Louth. This presents some interesting points: the Catholic Church, of course, did not change its very ancient ecclesiastic districts when the separate government was set up in Northern Ireland, so the part of Drogheda north of the Boyne is in the diocese of Armagh and enjoys the dispensation given so that meat can be eaten on Fridays on account of war conditions. A similar dispensation has been given throughout England. Drogheda in motion pictures and other matters is a rival town to Dundalk, which is further north and in the same county. Both are said to be good entertainment towns.

Next week, after my little trip to the west of Ireland, I am to meet with the members of the Theatrical and Cinema Association, to which most of the film exhibitors belong.

I was taken to lunch one day by Dan Terrell, the new press attaché at the American legation. I had met him some years ago when he was in charge of publicity and advertising for the Loew theatres in Washington. He said that he would be very glad to help if anything came up in motion-picture matters that he might assist with. He told me all about his most successful publicity stunt — perhaps you remember it – he had snowballs imported from Sun Valley for the August opening of Twentieth Century-Fox's 'Sun Valley Serenade' in Washington.

At the opening of the Dáil this week motion picture matters came up indirectly at one point in the debate, according to the newspaper reports. Mr Norton, leader of the Labour Party, in his attack or counter-attack (I don't know which) on Mr MacEntee, denounced campaign abuse directed against one of the Labour candidates, J. T. O'Farrell. Norton said that O'Farrell was accused of being an agent of freemasonry and had contacts with the communists, yet Mr Boland, the Minister of Justice, had appointed O'Farrell Chairman of the Appeal Board on film censorship, a post which O'Farrell had held for years. (As I pointed out, this appeal board functions only in matters concerned with morality; the war or political censorship cannot be appealed officially, though Mr Aiken may see and decide on any film.) Also on account of the election campaign I have not yet met O'Farrell. I hope to see him soon.

I have been reading *Challenge from Youth* by Father Devane, the Jesuit whom I mentioned in a previous letter. The book urges the formation of an Irish youth movement and contains extensive treatments of the youth movements in other nations, including the Axis countries. The following two sentences from the book might be of interest: 'When the people of this Christian State, Éire, strive to prevent imported pornography by Censorship of Films and Censorship of Publication Acts and to effect a moral cleansing similar to that in the USSR, so much lauded by the 'pinks' and the 'reds', they are scoffed at as reactionary puritans and killjoys and slayers of liberty by the 'high-brow' leftists in their midst . . . A modern state that cannot produce its own periodical secular literature and that does not make a portion of its own films scarcely deserves a name: the production of the former in Éire is relatively negligible and of the latter is practically nil.'

The excellent weather of the last couple of months continues.

PS On Saturday something happened that was very amusing and would have been criticised as unreal in a film: after driving a few miles the jarvey pulled up, on his own wish, before a pub and said the horse needed to draw his breath and he needed a pint of ale. So that was that.

12 July 1943
Dear Governor

This will cover the period July 5 to 10, during which I visited three fairly representative motion-picture cities in the west of Ireland – Galway, Limerick and Tralee, whose populations are about 20,000, 40,000 and 10,000, respectively.

In Galway I saw a number of interesting people, including the bishop, mayor, president of the university and of course all of the city's motion-picture exhibitors.

The Most Reverend Michael Browne, the bishop, very kindly saw me, even though he was on his annual retreat with the diocesan clergy at the local seminary, St Mary's College. A friend of Bishop Browne's in the US suggested that I make sure to meet him. After I arrived in Éire I learned that he was one of the more prominent members of the hierarchy so I was doubly anxious to see him. Bishop Browne met me at the entrance to the college (a place for philosophic and other basic training of the clergy in the diocese; he told me that the men go on to Maynooth for theology). He took me up to his study and then sat down comfortably in an easy chair and we had a grand conversation.

Bishop Browne said that he himself did not see many motion pictures. He remarked that it was a general view that the gangster and certain other types of films were not a good influence on children. The bishop, however, is not opposed to the American motion picture. In passing he said that he had made one trip out in 1930 and 'had left half his heart behind' when he returned.

In particular I asked Bishop Browne (as I did others on the trip) about the small but perhaps vigorous minority opposition to the American motion picture on the grounds that it spreads English and is a serious handicap to the campaign for the revival of Irish. His answer is significant because Galway is the capital of the chief native Gaelic-speaking area, with about 20 per cent able to speak and understand that language. Bishop Browne definitely said that he believed that such criticism of the motion picture meant nothing and should be disregarded. He further indicated that certain people are using the language for other purposes, for example as a way to get a job.

In the diocese of Galway, the bishop said, every priest must know Irish because in some parishes, even near the city, only Irish is used for sermons, etc. (I attended Mass one morning just a couple of minutes' walk from the Railroad Hotel and was somewhat surprised that the prayers after Mass were recited by the priest in Irish.)

Monsignor John Hines, President of the University of Galway, a part of the National University, was even stronger than the bishop in his comments dismissing opposition to the American motion picture on language grounds. He used the word 'humbug'. Monsignor Hines is a very charming, elderly man who, though keen as ever, is due for retirement. Like the bishop, he said that he did not see many films these days though he admitted frankly that when he did attend he preferred 'low-brow', action-type films. I saw Monsignor Hines with Mr Cullerton, manager of one of the three theatres in Galway. Monsignor Hines said that the students regularly attended Cullerton's theatre and the others. He also said that the college cooperated with the theatre managers by punishing any reported disturbance by students at the shows. Cullerton said they rarely had to report a student to the university authorities. Monsignor Hines said that students would be subject to a fine of perhaps a pound. (Monetary fines might improve discipline or order in US college towns with theatres.)

Some men, however, are extremely supportive of the Irish language and perhaps would carry the campaign for it even to opposing the English in motion pictures. (As a matter of fact, logically one should oppose motion pictures and anything else in the English language if it is seriously hoped to do away with English as the everyday spoken language of the majority of the people.) I had an interesting chat with Professor Liam O'Briain – professor of romance languages at Galway University and a man who is interested in many subjects, including motion pictures – after Cullerton introduced me to him.

Professor O'Briain admitted that, taking everything into consideration, the campaign for complete revival of the Irish language was impossible, but, he went on, the Irish rejoice in doing the impossible: 'that has been our history,' he said. Professor O'Brian has considerable interest in the future of a native Irish film industry.

I had quite a long visit with the Mayor of Galway, Joseph F. Costello: in fact his hospitality was amazing. I met him at the local Chamber of Commerce, where I was taken by Cullerton. The mayor invited us to a supper at the County Galway Club which consisted of a full-course dinner! The mayor also said that he did not attend pictures very often himself but, of course, always liked a good one. At the Galway Chamber of Commerce I was shown a newspaper clipping. The way the columnist – Kees van Hoek, a Dutchman who has travelled widely, including a year in New York, he said, to cover the Smith-Hoover campaign for a Dutch Catholic paper – writes, he should be working in Hollywood – he must have kissed the Blarney Stone repeatedly. I was naturally embarrassed when the Mayor of Galway pulled out of his pocket his daughter's autograph book and said she wanted mine. Can you imagine?

Cullerton also took me to see J. A. Power, the editor of

the chief papers in the area, the *Connaught Tribune* and the *Connaught Sentinel.* Power said that he only likes to see good films. His viewpoint on the language opposition to US films was similar to that of Monsignor Hines and the bishop. He remarked, apropos of this, that it was useless to try to understand the Irish because 'we can't understand ourselves'.

There are three theatres in Galway: the Savoy, managed by Cullerton and owned by a group headed by Walter McNally, RKO Radio Pictures distributor; the Estoria, managed by Mr Rafter and owned by Mr Mulligan, a solicitor in Ballina whom I hope to meet at a later date; and the Town Hall, owned by Mr Hardiman and run by his son. I had a visit with Hardiman Sr, who is now about seventy and retired on account of heart trouble. He told me that during the Troubles he was imprisoned in Wales with the present film censor, Dr Hayes. Young Hardiman later expressed regret that his father had never decided to build a new theatre. (Both the Savoy and the Estoria are fine, modern theatres and the Town Hall is ancient.) Although the Hardimans were in the theatre business for perhaps twenty years and more before the others in Galway, they now usually play second-run pictures.

In Limerick I had a long visit with Brian O'Brien, manager of the Grand Central Theatre and of the Goodwin china and glass store, which is owned by Mr Goodwin, who bought the theatre about seven years ago. O'Brien was new to the motion-picture business then but he had previously been successful in the other activity and since then had been successful in both. I also met Goodwin at his beautiful home just outside the city. O'Brien told me quite a bit about the attitude of the local clergy in Limerick towards motion pictures. Limerick is the only city or town – at least of any size – in the south of Ireland which does not show motion pictures on Sunday. (The theatres in other places, including Dublin, have two shows on Sunday, one at three in the afternoon and one at eight or eight thirty in the evening, closing down from about six to eight for the evening church services.) The attitude in Limerick appears to be rather unreasonable – dance halls and the like are permitted to operate. Some of the theatre men are anxious to open (here, as in the US, Sunday business is usually about a third that of the entire week) but others feel that the take in Limerick through the six days would be as good as spread over seven. In Limerick theatres they have a very good Monday, which is traditionally a poor business day, at least in America.

I was struck in Limerick by the fact that in Ireland the motion-picture theatre operator is regularly also engaged in some other activity. In Limerick, for example, Mr Cronin operates the Lyric Theatre and a pub which is frequented by many Americans and others awaiting clipper departures at Foynes; Mr Gough, who owns the Coliseum Theatre, is a prominent builder and contractor; the owner of the Carlton, Mr Williams, is in the related business of running amusements at county fairs and suchlike.

I called on Mr Cregan, editor of the *Limerick Leader*, and he told me that the people wanted 'clean films'. I believe I somewhat surprised him, as I like to do now, by pointing out that the American film producers are not as bad as is thought, giving the example of *Love on the Dole*, which passed the censor here and had great success but was refused a Film Code Seal in the US.

The manager of the Carlton, Mr Gafney, I believe, told

me about his wife's opinion that such American films as *The Dead End Kids* and the like should not be shown as they have – or may have? – a bad effect on children.

At the suggestion of Mr O'Curry, editor of the Catholic *Standard,* I called on Dan Doyle, the Limerick county librarian. Although he was not very interested in films, he talked about an art exhibition which he has recently mounted and showed me some figures of circulation of books through their main office in Limerick and the hundred branches in as many parishes which may be related to film-going. All types of books, with the exception of books on religion, books of literature or books in the Irish language, have increased in terms of reader interest in County Limerick over the past three years. The appeal of fiction has incraesed greatly; this should indicate continued or increased interest in motion pictures.

Also at the suggestion of O'Curry, endorsed by a couple of the Limerick exhibitors mentioned above, I tried to see Dr Cowper, the local priest, who is evidently the chief irritation on film matters locally. I called twice but did not see him. If he comes up to Dublin perhaps I can have a chat with him here.

In Tralee I spent a lot of time with Patrick Coffey, who operates the Picturedrome there and several other theatres in other towns, as well as being involved in the shoe business. Coffey made the interesting observation that in his opinion it was infinitely better to have the privileges of the clipper base at Foynes, etc., than have some of the war films passed by the censor. He evidently meant that in his opinion it was much better for the US and other countries to have landing facilities at Foynes than for him and other exhibitors to have available war-type motion pictures. I am sure no one would dispute that point if there were any relation between the two factors. Mr McSweeney, operator of the other theatre in Tralee, was away reopening a theatre in Bantry, but I had a good visit with Mr O'Shea, who runs McSweeney's theatre as well as being secretary of his general store.

From the brief trip I may make a few observations on the film tastes of the Irish people in those representative cities and towns of the west. (Eventually I hope to write at length on this subject in terms of the whole country.) According to my conversations with exhibitors in Galway, Limerick and Tralee the Irish motion-picture-goer in general likes the type of films which are most popular in America. Musicals are particular favourites here. Nelson Eddy and Jeanette MacDonald are very well liked. In common with people almost everywhere, the Irish like to laugh – a good comedy does very well, I was told. The people wish to forget, if they can, about the war when they go to a theatre, just as many people in America and other countries which are more directly affected by the war do. Although Ireland is neutral, the people here feel the war quite personally, I was told by the country exhibitors: almost every family has either a relation or good friend either in service or in war work in England. This is further extended by the well-known fact that practically everyone here has relations or intimate friends in the United States. That also makes people feel the effects of the war. One exhibitor told me that he and the people in his theatre 'felt almost like weeping when the films of Pearl Harbour were shown. It was just like your own flesh and blood.'

Despite everything, however, the theatre business is very

good indeed. While pictures are scarce and film rentals said to be high, evidently the exhibitors are doing reasonably well. For example, last night in Tralee I was in a theatre which seats 1,000 (large for a town of 10,000) and two old and poor pictures were being shown, yet the house was packed.

I was agreeably surprised that I was able to make the trip so pleasantly. The trains, of course, are restricted and quite crowded but nevertheless satisfactory. Of course I had a very grand reception from the various film people I met. By the way, if you are ever in the southern tip of Ireland remember Benner's Hotel, Tralee, which is said to have the best food in Ireland. I left there this morning shortly after eight and got back to Dublin at about six.

I learned on the trip that the government here, to encourage stage productions, does not charge any admission tax on stage shows or mixed programs when the stage part exceeds the length of the film shown. This leads to some interesting special stage and screen shows occasionally in certain provincial theatres. In the US, of course, the entertainment tax is collected on all forms. Here there is frank discrimination against the motion picture in favor of the stage.

17 July 1943
Dear Governor
This will cover the week of July 12 to 17.

As I mentioned previously, I delayed submitting my letters of introduction to Sean T. O'Kelly and Frank Aiken until after the election and opening of the new Dáil. I saw both this week.

I am enclosing the letter from O'Kelly's office; it is the first written in the Irish official style which I have received. O'Kelly was most pleasant. He said that he sees very few films: probably not more than a half dozen since he became a minister eleven years ago. He also said that, although before that time he was fond of the theatre, he has not seen more than a couple of plays since he became a minister. He is so busy that he works almost every evening on something to do with his government position and does not have time for theatrical recreation. O'Kelly, of course, has many friends in the US, having made about a dozen trips there, and naturally he has a general interest in the motion picture. He indicated that there is considerable difference of opinion about film censorship – some believe it is not strict enough and others that it is too strict. He pointed out that the special problems here in Ireland make a special type of film censorship necessary.

Aiken invited me to lunch on Thursday. He had with him Frank Gallagher, head of the government's Information Bureau. Mr Aiken explained in detail the reasons for the strict film censorship. The basic position evidently is that now the people of Éire are all united on the position of neutrality and it is desired that nothing be shown on a theatre screen which might disturb that unity in any way. The censorship then may be said to look inwards rather than outwards. That is, the reasons for its operation are essentially internal ones and not, as in the other neutral countries, chiefly aimed at avoiding anything that might seriously annoy a belligerent nation. Aiken said that he did not believe any of the belligerents cared what was shown on the picture screens here but the Irish government wished to avoid any disturbances in the cinemas. As an example, Aiken said that in one cinema a pro-British woman started to applaud a picture of British ARP services in action, which of themselves were innocuous. Others in the audience started to boo and hiss as a protest against the un-neutral applauding of this woman. She, he said, misinterpreted this reaction as an unsympathetic one to the suffering depicted in the scenes.

Aiken, I believe, personally rather likes motion pictures, especially the good ones. As I previously reported, he is the informal but official and deciding appeal on Emergency Powers Order cuts required by the film censor. He said that he had seen about half a dozen pictures in this connection. (I understand from the renters that several pictures are now awaiting his inspection. During recent weeks, with the election campaign, he did not have time to watch them.) Mr Aiken asked quite a few questions about motion pictures. There is, as you know, hope of establishing an industry here. He said that he thought that perhaps in ten years' time the Irish language would be suitable for films shown in this country. He expressed interest in the relative lack of American historical films, suggesting that a really good picture on the life of George Washington should have great appeal.

Mr Gallagher has a special interest in educational and cultural films. I pointed out to them, as I have done on several occasions here, that on account of the war censorship, which rejects so many of the best current films, there is now a distorted impression in Ireland of the American motion picture. I mentioned that the best stars, writers, directors and producers are in many cases now put in films which have at least some kind of current war background. Aiken said he knew that many fine pictures were being missed here now but that they were content to wait until after the war for these films' public exhibition in this country. (Of course no one knows whether there will be a market for such pictures after the war.)

This week I had the educational approach to motion pictures, from the Irish point of view, explained well by Senator Liam O'Buachalla (William Buckley) of Galway. Senator O'Buachalla is an economist, educator and head of learned societies here. He is very interested in the future of visual education, which involves using motion pictures for many types of instruction. Senator O'Buachalla also pointed out that Éire must be viewed in a different light than any other neutral and that comparisons of film matters in other neutral nations were not suitable. He pointed out that on account of the short history of the nation as a self-governing country, certain things must be done here to help revive the national culture. This movement even extends to motion pictures. He admitted and justified from his point of view a 'leaning over backwards'. He drew a comparison with patients who were convalescent. These persons naturally do not know what is best for them and must follow the doctor's instructions and decisions: And so it is with this country in the decisions which have been and should be made on films. (Senator O'Buachalla pointed out that some people did not think that the film censorship was strict enough, especially from the angle of films which do not promote the ideals which are believed to be compatible with the culture of the country.) The films made in America are viewed by some as a threat to the native traditions. Senator O'Buachalla believes that there should be an international body such as a committee of the League of Nations which would assemble data from all over the world on what should and should not be included in films. He said that motion pictures can be a threat to the moral, cultural and economic standards of other countries.

The action of the Gaelic Athletic Association in banning certain sports was cited by the senator as a type of the 'leaning over backwards' which he viewed as essential to restore the Irish tradition in that field. From others I learned a bit more about the historical reasons for the sports bans which makes it easier to understand them, though it does not explain the reason for their application during the last twenty-five years. It seems, according to some, that certain sports, from the Irish point of view, were linked inseparably with British rule and those who carried out that rule. In a very practical way it was asserted that various sports were steps which often led Irishmen into friendships and ultimately some form of service, perhaps in the British Army. So far as I know, the Gaelic Athletic Association has not continued its ban of certain sports into a ban of films in which the sports appear, but anything is possible. I believe that the league, in a very authoritarian way, is not only against certain sports but even forbids a member to spectate at any of the banned sports.

On Tuesday I was invited to speak at a meeting of the Theatrical and Cinema Association, an exhibitors' organisation. After explaining in detail the purpose of my visit here I spoke for a while on certain aspects of motion picture public relations. The motion picture theatre operators here seemed interested in the suggestion that they should seriously concern themselves with the general esteem and prestige of the motion picture here. I noted that since I arrived I have followed the press carefully for comments on motion pictures and quite generally the references were unfriendly, very frequently as a result of ignorance of certain film matters. Here the motion picture does not appear to be as highly regarded in religious, educational and government circles as it should be, or as it is in the US and other countries.

Dr Hayes, the film censor, is away on vacation. Michael J. Dolan, his deputy, is 'leaning way over backwards' as he does not wish to make the slightest mistake. He rejected in one week three films from one company and ordered numerous cuts, some most trivial and silly. The film renters will welcome the return of Dr Hayes, as strict as he is.

Louis Elliman, who operates motion-picture theatres, a distributing company and a stage theatre, was telling me last night that officially there is not censorship of the stage and things are permitted which are not allowed in films, but the presentation of a play such as *The Watch on the Rhine* or *The Moon is Down* would be stopped, probably just before the opening. It seems that films come in for the strictest censorship of all. Aiken told me that the censorship of the press need not be so strict because if a person does not like a newspaper story he need not read it but in a cinema he may create a disturbance.

24 July 1943
Dear Governor

This will cover the period of July 19 to 24.

The Theatre and Cinema Association of Ireland gave a luncheon this week at which I was the guest. About thirty members of the film business here, including distributors and exhibitors, were present. Also the new Lord Mayor of

Dublin, Martin O'Sullivan, was there. He, like many other officials and prominent individuals in this country, is not familiar with motion pictures. He remarked that he sees very few of them. I believe that will probably change because, now that he is lord mayor, he will be invited to many film openings and the like. He was very pleasant and struck me as a person who would like motion pictures if he saw half a dozen or so good ones. He made a nice, brief speech and showed that he was a man who can pick up very quickly basic points of a more or less complex business.

I was pleasantly surprised when J. M. Stanley, introducing me, spoke first in Irish. (Stanley, as I believe I have previously mentioned operates several theatres in the Boyne area and publishes the *Drogheda Argus*.) Although very few present understood Stanley's speech until he himself translated, it was a nice gesture. Stanley knows Irish well but is not part of the small minority which would like to ban everything in English, including films. While almost everyone will tell you about the part he played in the Troubles (there must have been many people in the GPO in 1916), Stanley was very active, getting out the newspaper for the Irish forces in a nearby printing establishment which had been requisitioned.

When I was called upon, I spoke in general terms because the gathering was a mixture of exhibitors and renters and the occasion was primarily a social one. I thanked the Theatre and Cinema Association for the tribute to the American motion-picture industry, etc. I then said something that was probably not known widely (if at all) here before: that Dublin had an intimate connection with what was to be the modern motion picture as far back as 250 years ago. I mentioned that a citizen of Dublin who was also an Irish patriot, William Molyneux, was the first to describe in the English language the magic lantern, the basic device for screen entertainment. I had learned that fact during my research in the US on the prehistory of the motion picture. I had a chance to verify the fact before the luncheon by seeing a copy of Molyneux's book *Dioptrica Nova*, published in 1692, in Trinity College Library.

At the luncheon I was seated between Gerald Ellis, this year's president of the Theatre & Cinema Association, and Maurice Elliman, the dean of exhibitors here and, I believe, the first head of the association. Elliman, who is now a good age but is still very active in the business, told me how he came here from Lithuania, then a part of Russia, and started in the film business in 1910. Before that he was getting only seven and sixpence a week. He toured Éire with a combination show of a picture made of a big English prize fight and four live boxers who put on fights for the audience. From that start, he grew in the business here to the point where his operations and those of his sons are the chief ones in the cinema business in this country. The Ellimans own a few cinemas and operate a few more. They also own the Gaiety stage theatre. One of Elliman's sons, Louis, runs most of the business, including managing one of the firms that distributes American films. He handles Republic pictures. Another son manages the largest theatre in Ireland – the Theatre Royal, which has both stage presentations and a picture on the same bill, as at the Music Hall or Paramount theatres in New York. A couple of other sons are also in the business here and a couple more are in the British forces overseas. Ellis manages the Savoy Cinema, which is operated by the Ellimans and is the biggest exclusively motion-picture theatre in Ireland.

Louis Elliman took me to see a new Irish play being presented at the Gaiety theatre this week. It is called *The Dingle Republic* and concerns events which took place during 1921 and 1922, the Civil War period, in the extreme western tip of County Kerry. The author, Edward Sheehy, a character who wears quite a beard, has, I believe, aspirations for production of his works on Broadway and possibly in Hollywood. I doubt that the current play would have much interest in the US. As a matter of fact the play has been attracting the smallest audiences in a very long time to the theatre, according to Elliman. While everyone who took part in the strife which the play depicts would perhaps not agree with everything said in the play, an outsider like myself would think that there should be great interest in such a subject. One of the newspaper reviews, in the *Irish Press,* said that, had the play been produced in the 1922–30 period, there would have been a riot in the theatre. Elliman said, of course, that they would never have put on the play had they known that there would be no disturbance since emotions have died down. On the other hand, the lack of interest in the play came as a surprise to them.

I saw W. T. Cosgrave this week. Pat Casey, the motion-picture producers' labour contact in Hollywood, had given me an introduction to him but as in the case of introductions to Aiken and O'Kelly I waited until after the election and reopening of the new Dáil before trying to see him. Of course he is pretty well along in years now but was very pleasant. Like many of the other officials I have written to you about, he sees very few pictures. In fact he mentioned that the last he had seen was *Citizen Kane.* He saw that in a party at the film censor's office. (As I believe I may have written before, the film censor sometimes invites some of the government officials and their wives to attend the screening of what he knows is an interesting film.) I asked Cosgrave about his opinion on the opposition to the American motion picture on the grounds that it was in English. Like the Bishop of Galway and others, he dismissed that position, although he is of course very much in favour of the Irish-language revival. I saw Cosgrave at his office at the Fine Gael Party headquarters.

At the suggestion of a priest friend of mine and a very close friend of a priest in New York I called on the High Commissioner for Canada, John D. Kearney. I told Kearney about my work in connection with the study of film censorship here and the film tastes of Irish audiences and remarked that the only subject of Canadian interest which has come up in American films since I arrived was the 'March of Time' issue of *The New Canada*.

Michael J. Dolan, an actor with the Abbey Theatre, is continuing as film censor in the absence of Dr Hayes. As any deputy might be expected to be, Dolan is very strict. In fact the companies feel he is much too strict and some are scheduling pictures so they will come up for censorship following the return of Dr Hayes on the first of August. Dolan is evidently cutting the word 'war' itself, no matter how it is used, and so on. I have not been at the film censor's office very frequently since Dr Hayes started his vacation. I recently saw at a cinema *Aloma of the South Seas*. Although certain moral objections to it were raised by Dr Hayes, who is very much against South American- and South Seas-type dancing, the film was passed by the appeal board. I had lunch today with Mrs Fitzgerald, who has been a member of the appeal board since it was established, about twenty years ago. She appears to take a reasonable position.

Next week I plan to spend a day in Kilkenny and divide the rest of the week between Waterford and Cork. I received a telephone invitation to meet the Cork film exhibitors at lunch on Friday.

22 July 1943, Exhibition in Ireland

The motion-picture exhibitor in Ireland, the only English-speaking neutral nation in the present war, has many of the problems of his contemporaries in belligerent countries and also faces certain circumstances peculiar to this country.

At present, the most serious difficulty of the motion-picture industry in Ireland is the war censorship. This is a matter of considerable concern to the distributors (called 'renters' in this country and England) and to the exhibitors. A fairly serious product shortage has already resulted and reissues and return engagements are commonplace.

The basic aim of the war censorship of films is to keep off theatre screens any picture or scene which might cause any audience disturbance. This makes the censorship stricter here than in the other neutral country. There is, naturally, no agreement on the part of the renters or exhibitors with all the cuts or rejections ordered by the film censor. Most people here in the motion-picture industry recognise, however, that it would be best to avoid anything that would cause trouble.

There is a tradition in Ireland of violent action even in such matters as a few motion pictures which were considered objectionable by some. The actual cases of serious audience trouble, even over a period of twenty years, are few in number, but exhibitors or renters who have been in the business for a considerable length of time can recall cases when the film was taken out and publicly burned. Most of these occurrences were concerned with pictures held to be pro-British. That has not applied in all cases, though. For example an exhibitor in Limerick City told the writer that years ago one of the Martin Johnson African travel films (edited by Terry Ramsaye, the editor of *Motion Picture Herald*) was seized at the theatre and destroyed by private individuals.

The small-town exhibitor in Ireland, unlike the majority in the United States, is regularly a man who divides his time between the operation of his theatre and some other business. This is even so in many cases where the motion-picture-theatre interests are quite important, extending to daily operation in several different towns. Hence in many cases the provincial exhibitor is a man of prominence in his community who is aware of his civic responsibilities.

Certain Irish film exhibitors are also proprietors and managers of many types of businesses, including pubs, general stores, newspaper publishing and printing businesses, shoe manufacturing, hotels, building and contracting and many other enterprises. In some instances exhibitors here are also politicians, schoolteachers and, strangest of all, priests.

Several of the most prominent theatre operators are also in the restaurant business, running cafés where everything from a cup of tea to a full course dinner is served. These café-restaurants are associated with most of the first-run theatres in Dublin and with a number of the more important theatres in other large cities.

In certain places the café-restaurant run in conjunction with the motion-picture house is a more profitable enterprise than the theatre itself. Everywhere the joint operation is maintained it is believed that there is a certain amount of mutual help between the two businesses. Although the house may be crowded and the café empty, and vice versa, depending on the picture, the weather and other circumstances, a good eating place right in the theatre building provides an excellent meeting place for picture patrons, and those who have had a pleasant meal or light refreshment may quite easily be tempted to drop in to see the picture.

The Irish exhibitor is usually burdened by a greater range of admission prices than his American counterpart. Most picture houses here have at all times three different price seats for adults. The best seats are those in the front balcony and the scale ranges from about one shilling four pence (about thirty cents) in the provincial towns to two shillings six pence (about fifty cents) in first runs in Dublin. The second-best seats are those in the rear half or two-thirds of the orchestra and the cheapest seats are in the front of the house. The minimum runs down to about sevenpence in the evening and fourpence in the afternoon in small towns (about twelve and seven cents, respectively).

Most theatres in Ireland operate seven days a week (with the exception of Limerick, where motion pictures are not allowed to be shown on Sundays). All theatres which operate on Sundays must close down in the early evening in order not to conflict with church services, however. Likewise, no pictures are allowed on Sunday morning. This means that theatres open for one matinée show on Sunday and close at about 5.30 or 6 pm and reopen at 8 or 8.30. For the Sunday-evening show, the best business of the week, seats are reserved in advance in the important theatres. This, of course, means extra work for the exhibitor, as numbered tickets must be issued and a considerable house staff must be available to seat properly all the patrons, who arrive at about the same time.

The Irish government's entertainment tax is directed especially at the motion picture and special exemption is given to stage productions. Regular stage plays pay no admission tax. If a theatre runs motion pictures and stage presentations on the same bill the government charges no admission tax if the stage part of the show is longer than the film fare. Chiefly on account of this factor, certain larger provincial-town theatres run occasional stage presentations. Strictly speaking, here in Ireland the word 'theatre' is applied only to places where stage shows only or stage shows and films are presented; the conventional motion picture house is a 'cinema'.

The Irish exhibitor has this most vital factor in common with the American exhibitor: generally the audiences like the same types of motion pictures. Films which are box office successes in the US are regularly extremely popular in Éire. On account of this, the industry here regrets the loss of so many films of a war-background type which have been hits in America and have been rejected or seriously cut by the Irish Film Censor. Musicals, action pictures and comedies (provided the latter are not too sophisticated) are special favorites of Irish audiences. Colour films are also good attractions.

The Shelbourne Hotel, Dublin, 14 August 1943
Dear Governor

This will cover the week of August 9 to 14.

As I believe I have mentioned previously, the film censor's

office in Éire is officially under the Department of Justice, but since 1942 appeals on war cuts ordered in films go to Mr Aiken as Minister for the Coordination of Defensive Measures. Any appeals on moral grounds go to a regular appeal board set up for the purpose.

I had an appointment with Gerald Boland, Minister for Justice. Boland explained that, although the film censor's office is under his department, it functions pretty well on its own and personally he sees rather few films. He said that he has seen a number of the problem pictures at the film censor's office since the beginning of the war. In general, Boland indicated that he likes most films he sees though he only goes unofficially when members of his own family tell him that such and such is a very good film which he should see. He said that he had heard some criticism of the motion picture on the alleged grounds that films have an influence on juvenile crime, etc.

Boland explained the reasons for the strict film censorship at present, pointing to the history of the country. (As I have indicated previously, much of the current censorship of films is to prevent any disturbance or applause and hissing in any cinema. This might come from some people objecting to a scene or objecting to the favorable reaction of certain persons in the audience, it is said. For example, some might applaud a scene of Churchill; others would object to the scene and so object to the applause.) Boland indicated that he believed there was more need now than at any previous time for very strict film censorship. Like others, Boland dismissed the 'language' objection to American films.

Had a long chat with Frank Robbins, secretary of the theatre and cinema section of the Irish Transport and General

Workers Union. All cinema employees in Dublin and the other chief cities are members. I was especially interested to get his reactions because the members of the union would be the first to face any audience or any other kind of cinema disturbance. Robbins said that there was a possibility of trouble if certain scenes or pictures were shown but he believed the present film censorship is too strict. Like many others here, he does not see very many pictures. His sixteen-year-old son is a fan and wrote, unknown to his father, a paper on the cinema which got the highest mark in his class and has been favorably commented on by some people in the film business and by two of the judges who have been concerned about the question of the film and its effects on the young. Robbins's son took the view, accepted in America but perhaps not here, that films do not cause juvenile delinquency. Robbins told me all about the apprenticeship course for motion picture operators. The youngsters attend a trades school during part of their working week and must complete a set course in between three and five years. He believes that the city and town projectionists in Ireland are the best in Europe. I was glad to learn that the union official concerned with films seemed rather satisfied with general conditions. Of course the film business here, like everywhere else, pays relatively good wages, etc.

In my letter covering July 26 to August 1, I referred to a speech by Professor A. O'Rahilly of Cork University that criticised cinemas in rural Ireland. I wrote to him about that, attaching a copy of the motion-picture production code. Professor O'Rahilly wrote a letter in reply which said in part: 'I am afraid my view is that profit-run commercial cinemas (and dance halls) in the villages and countryside are undesirable. The topics would be completely sophisticated and urbanised. They would not cater for the real education of people who lack the facilities of town. They would hold out false ideals to people unable to be critical of them. Besides, the 16 mm films can be produced cheaply and can be exhibited by travelling apparatus in out-of-the-way places where Hollywood productions would not pay. Can't you be content with the cities and towns? I am not being dogmatic about all this, of course. I am merely expressing my ideal.'

Professor O'Rahilly, I am told, is doing very fine work in connection with adult education but I believe the standards he is setting for film entertainment are too high. From our point of view, the people in rural areas have just as much right to fine film entertainment as those in towns. In fact, provision of satisfactory amusement in the country should be a powerful factor in keeping people on the farms, which appears to be a very serious problem in this country.

The *Irish Times* this morning had an interesting editorial, entitled 'The Cinema's Influence', which relates to this subject. One good thought included in it was that: 'An adult citizen, who is deemed responsible enough to cast a vote to determine the future of his nation, is surely responsible enough to maintain his balance before the productions of Hollywood. He views them as entertainment, not as ideals.'

On the other hand, the position of those − of whom there are unfortunately too many − who are opposed to American motion pictures is summed up in a pamphlet called *National Action - A Plan for the National Recovery of Ireland,* published under the pseudonym of Joseph Anelius by the Gaelic Athletic Association. The author is a layman, a writer by the name of Hanlon or Hanley. I was first curious why such a pamphlet would be published by the athletic association but was told it was done to secure an immediate, fairly broad sale and because the association put up the funds needed for printing. It said on films:

'We must establish our own Cinema or Film Service for the production of films for home use, together with educational, historic and other useful films from abroad. Apart from its industrial aspect, home-produced films depicting real Irish life, modern and historic, would give to ourselves, and to the world, for the first time, a true representation of this country. This is necessary for retaining the goodwill of even our own people abroad. They are often ashamed of the garbled, distorted, stage-Irish and sometimes vindictive way in which the country is misrepresented. The Christian, social, economic and national demoralizing influences of the present flood of foreign films of inferior type which afflict this country are incalculable – pictures extolling idleness, extravagance, superficiality and depravity of all kinds. All the small countries of Europe had to fight this battle against nationally demoralizing films; we must do the same or surrender entirely to them. To cut out this deadly, creeping poison, to establish ourselves, even in our own estimation, as a distinct community, and in numerous other important ways, a National Film Producing Service is a vitally essential feature of a National Recovery Plan.'

A bit of film production for Éire for next year has been announced in the press – a front-page story. The plan is to film the outdoor scenes here and the studio shots in London (the latter being much the greater part of the production). A budget of £120,000 has been announced: since that is a dozen times what it could probably take in this country, the film is obviously intended primarily for circulation abroad. People in the film business here point out that there is a big difference between announcing something and accomplishing it.

Dr Hayes, the film censor, had me to dinner at his home one evening this week. He has a charming wife, and the couple have three children. Other guests were B. Y. McPeake, who was born here but raised in England and is managing director of the Cosmopolitan (Hearst) magazines in England, and Dr and Mrs Burke: Dr Burke is a great collector of all things Irish.

This week I saw *Mission to Moscow* (Warner Bros.). Have not heard officially but believe it will be rejected. The whole cabinet attended a screening of the picture. Even if there was nothing to do with the war in it, it would probably be rejected because, as you know, here they pretty much ignore the existence of Russia. *Flight for Freedom* (RKO) is now playing in a first-run theatre. I dropped in to see the end and beginning of it: although not much footage has been cut, several important parts to the story are missing, so the audience has little idea what the whole thing is about.

Had an interesting visit with Father R. S. Devane SJ. As others have done, he pointed out the need for strict film censorship and based his argument on historical grounds. He wants more moral US films but admitted that he does not see very many and prefers European pictures. He also remarked that priests here are not allowed to go to stage theatres. (The regulation applies to priests stationed in the various dioceses here and not to the visitors, etc.) It is a strange rule because the stage plays here are almost always entirely 'clean' and it would seem important that priests know what the public is seeking in way of plays as in the case of pictures. In Dublin and some of the other towns, priests regularly attend the cinema. I hope that practice extends everywhere in this country: it should result in fewer attacks against films. The church here is, of course, very conservative and 'makes haste slowly'.

Mr O'Curry, editor of the Catholic *Standard*, invited me to the dinner given in honor of John Betjeman, the departing British Press Attaché. O'Curry mentioned that he was thrilled by the first real play he saw – it was at the Abbey Theatre just after he withdrew from Maynooth Seminary. I thought that a true and interesting observation and questioned him about the ban for priests here; I asked him why he does not conduct a campaign for its removal. He did not seem to think that such a rule of the church here would be changed very quickly.

I showed the Canadian High Commissioner here the cuts made by the film censor in the 'March of Time' issue of *The New Canada,* which I have mentioned previously. He was interested but diplomatic, as I expected.

This week I spoke with a number of exhibitors and renters, including Neville of MGM; Livingstone of Twentieth Century-Fox; Nashe of Warners; Knight, a cinema operator in Athlone; Tallon, the owner of a cinema in Cork and a partner in cinemas in Galway and Waterford and Jones, Ellis and Farrell, Dublin exhibitors. I also talked with A. D. Baker, the RCA sound engineer for Éire.

London, 23 August 1943
Dear Governor
This will cover the week of August 16 to 21. On Friday August 20 I crossed over from Dublin to London.

In Dublin during the week I saw three interesting short subjects in the 'This Is America' series (RKO Radio). In the first, *Boomtown, USA,* (Washington), a reference to Washington as the headquarters of the United Nations and a short shot of President Roosevelt were cut. The second film, *Air Crew,* showed the training of a naval flying team. The third was on the doctor shortage in the US. I believe that those two films passed substantially without cuts. The Columbia picture *The More the Merrier* was cut substantially, on moral grounds. The company will probably appeal, and the film has a good chance of passing the appeal board without cuts. I also saw the Twentieth-Century Fox film *Crash Dive* at a pre-censorship private screening at the Royal Theatre. It should pass with only very minor cuts.

Joseph Martin, United Artists manager and a pioneer in the film business in Ireland, explained the origin of the film censor's office. After the establishment of the Free State, all of the various local councils exercised the right of film censorship and the industry was running into a chaotic situation: films would be passed in one town and banned in another. In some cases the film would be taken from a theatre and publicly burned by the local authorities. Representatives of the film business went to Kevin O'Higgins, who was then Minister for Justice. He told the delegation that the government would be glad to help but did not have the money to set up a central film censorship, so the companies worked out a licence fee for the censoring expenses. It was agreed that any profit made would be refunded. (This has never happened.) Local bodies cannot interfere with films licensed by the state censor, but the film censor's office functions as a more or less independent government agency that is only loosely attached to the Department of Justice.

Had an interesting chat with Roisin Walsh, chief librarian of the Dublin public libraries, whom the government sent on a tour of the US in the spring of 1939 to learn about American feelings towards Ireland. I was surprised to learn that the censorship does not prohibit the circulation of 'war' books, as 'war' films are stopped. Many of the books that are popular at the libraries are British war records or accounts of various kinds. Walsh is a director of the Irish Film Society and, being interested in education, is probably personally opposed to the strict film censorship. She is anxious that I meet other directors of the Film Society so that they can discuss the question and determine whether there is anything they can do to ease the situation.

Leo McCauley, Irish Consul General in New York, now home on a couple of months' holiday, had me to his home on Wednesday evening. He is very charming. I met his sister, a brother and a few of his friends. McCauley said he would like to come with me to the film censor's office some day and meet Dr Hayes. I shall have to arrange that when I return to Dublin. Having resided in New York for a number of years, McCauley is quite familiar with motion pictures.

On Tuesday evening I had another interesting dinner with J. M. Stanley, Drogheda exhibitor and newspaper publisher. We discussed chiefly the future of television in relation to motion-picture-theatre operation. Other exhibitors with whom I had long talks during the week included Mr Farrell, general manager of the Capitol Theatre Company, which runs about six first-run cinemas, including the Capitol, and several so-called working-class halls in poorer areas of Dublin, and Jack Ellis, operator of the first-run Carlton

Cinema on O'Connell Street and owner of the Grafton, which used to be the 'swanky' cinema of Dublin.

I obtained the British permit and the Irish reentry visa on Wednesday. Plane reservations must be made two weeks in advance, I discovered, so I came over by boat. At that I was not able to obtain a 'sailing ticket' at the steamship office but obtained one through Paramount. In order to control the number of passengers each day the company issues 'sailing tickets' in addition to the ordinary ticket. The trip from Dublin to London these days is long and not very pleasant. The weather was bad and the sea rough. Fortunately I was not seasick but hundreds of the passengers were. One feels very sorry for the many women travelling with small children. The train part of the journey was pleasant enough but very long. The boat train left Dublin at 7.20 am and we did not arrive at Euston Station, London until 8.30 pm.

On Saturday I called in at Mr Allport's office, and his secretary, Miss Maitland, was there. She told me that at the last meeting of the managing directors at the association's office she mentioned to Mr Eckman that I was coming over for a visit and he said they would have to call a meeting so that I can talk to all the interested company men at the same time. This morning (Monday) I was also in at the office and we tried to reach Mr Eckman by phone but he was on the way to London from the country. I expect to hear from him later.

30 August 1943
Dear Governor

This will cover the week of August 23 to 28.

I got in touch with Sam Eckman, managing director of

Metro-Goldwyn-Mayer, just before he left for New York. He told me over the phone that Joseph Friedman, managing director of Columbia Pictures, was serving as chairman of the group of American film companies here in his absence. I spoke to Friedman then. Arrangements were made to hold a group meeting of the American company representatives at Allport's office. His secretary set a time which was convenient for everyone. The meeting was held on Thursday morning at Allport's office.

At the meeting, which lasted an hour and a half, I gave a complete report on my findings in connection with film matters in Ireland, notably censorship during the Emergency. I made a few recommendations, chief among which was that the companies send as many of their films as possible to Éire, even films which they believe will certainly be rejected by the film censor. The reason for this is that the censorship is not very consistent and, in advance, it can never be known exactly what will be rejected; furthermore I feel it is good policy, from a psychological point of view, to let the film censor see even the violently anti-Nazi films (which frequently are very well made). When the censor realises how powerful some of the anti-Nazi films are, he may be inclined to pass over some little things in other films which might appear to him to be important if he has no standard of comparison.

It is likely that I shall see various of the individual company representatives later to talk about any matters directly concerning their films in Éire. Most of the week, however, was spent writing up a fairly extensive report on the film situation there.

Shortly after I arrived in London last weekend, I was

advised that it would be a good idea for me to see representatives of the three motion-picture trade papers published
here. It was thought, doubtless correctly, that if I did not
speak to the trade press they would feel free to write whatever
they felt about my visit to Éire and film censorship there.
Aubrey Flanagan and Hope Williams Burnup, the Quigley
Publications editor and manager, were present when I saw
the trade press and it all turned out very well. The three
papers published friendly little items which did not include
anything that might disturb the film censor in Éire or
interfere with my future relations with him.

The weather has been reasonably good lately.

6 September 1943
Dear Governor

This will cover the period of August 30 to September 4.

During the week I saw Joseph Friedman, managing
director of Columbia Pictures; J. Walton Brown, general sales
manager, Warner Bros.; J. Arthur Rank, chief British film
magnate; Frank Ditcham, managing director of General Film
Distributors, which handles Universal pictures; William
Garling, RCA Photophone engineer; and Jack Beddington,
head of the films division of the British Ministry of
Information. I also spent a day at the Denham Studios, the
largest studios in England.

I told Beddington about the current film situation in Éire,
especially in reference to the censorship. The only concrete
suggestion I had for him was that perhaps he might consider
proposing that the English newsreel companies resume
providing a newsreel service in Éire. John Betjeman, for
several years British Press Attaché in Dublin and now back at

the films division in London, was also there, and Beddington asked him whether any consideration should be given to Éire in the matter of a newsreel. Mr Betjeman said that some consideration should be given because about 1 million Irish citizens have relatives in the British services. Then Beddington asked that I prepare some notes on what the film censor in Éire may or may not pass in the way of newsreels. He said he would have Betjeman come to his next meeting with the British newsreel group and discuss the matter.

Arthur Rank had an interesting story about the Irish. Although he has controlling interests in every phase of the British film business, the Rank's family's chief holdings are flour mills. Rank said his firm has a third of the milling business in Éire. He remarked that ten or twelve years ago the Irish government ruled that all flour sold in Éire had to be milled there. One of the British milling companies lost about £1 million of business goodwill in Éire, Rank said, because they did not open up new mills there. That company asked the government for a licence to operate the new mill and the Irish government said, 'Put up the mill first and then we will talk about the licence.' Rank said the same statement was made to him in connection with a new mill for Limerick, but he said he guessed, correctly, that the Irish government did not actually mean what one would interpret from those words. He put up the new mill and applied for the licence to operate it; the licence was immediately granted with no trouble whatsoever. The moral of the story was that people who speak the same language – as Americans, English and Irish do – frequently find that this is a handicap because they think they know what the others mean by certain statements and are sometimes entirely wrong. If different languages were involved, people would not be tempted to think they always knew what the other fellow had in mind.

Brown, Warner's general sales manager, told me that he considers Dublin to be the most profitable motion-picture city of its size anywhere. Friedman was inclined to take the position that business there mattered little. When all the companies' business is included the sum is not insignificant. Ditcham was very interested in censorship details in Éire. He said that he had considered making a special newsreel for Éire but had decided it would be too much trouble. Garling showed me RCA sound installations in two representative London theatres, the Warner and the Empire. At the Denham studio the chief picture being worked on is *Henry V,* for which outdoor scenes were shot in Éire (the first major company scenes ever made there).

I met also Robert Littlewood, a veteran drama and motion-picture reviewer. One of his current jobs might be considered quite Irish: he is the motion-picture critic for the *Belfast Telegraph* but has never been to Belfast and writes some of the reviews from the *Motion Picture Herald.* It seems the newspaper lets him know which pictures are to play in Belfast, and then, in London, he writes reviews for the Belfast readers. If he has not seen the picture he looks up the *Herald* review. Great system.

Saw a couple of plays – *Flare Path* and *Watch on the Rhine* – which I had missed in New York. Also saw the long British film *The Life and Death of Colonel Blimp.* It is about an hour too long (it runs nearly three hours) but is quite good. I could not see why some people here are against exporting the film to the US.

6 September 1943, British Newsreels in Éire
To John Betjeman of the Ministry of Information's film
division, London
Dear Mr Betjeman

As requested on Friday afternoon, I have typed out a few
notes on newsreel service for Éire. I hope they will give you
some of the information for which you are looking.

If Mr Beddington proposes to the newsreel companies that
they do something about Éire and a plan is worked out, I shall
be glad – if you wish – to discuss details of what would and
would not be acceptable with Mr Aiken and Dr Hayes.

From every point of view I think it is regrettable that
Éire has been without any newsreel for several months now.
The Irish should be shown – I know the cinema patrons
want to be shown – as much of what is happening as possible.
From a business point of view it seems to me that a newsreel
is an essential part of a film show.

Best wishes.

Newsreel Service for Éire
Early in the war it was found that most of the scenes included
in the British newsreels were rejected by the Irish film censor.

Until early this spring, three of the newsreel companies
carried on distribution in Éire with a joint newsreel
composed in part of scenes taken by a cameraman in Éire
and in part of non-war general subjects. This newsreel was
discontinued on the grounds that there was not raw film
stock available for the special reel. The decision was generally
welcomed by the Irish exhibitors, who had long since tired
of the many zoo and other animal scenes which comprised
much of the issues.

Several war scenes were passed by the film censor before distribution of the special newsreel was halted. These included the Japanese attack on Pearl Harbour and an attack on an aircraft carrier in the Pacific. The Irish public rushed to see these newsreels.

It is possible and would be worthwhile, I believe, to make up a special newsreel for Éire which could include a substantial amount of 'war' scenes. It is likely that there is ample general and war material to make up at least one reel a week for Éire. The scenes would have to be selected with regard to Irish film censorship, and in particular the commentary would have to be neutral, from the Irish point of view, as observation of Irish film censorship shows that it is regularly the commentary and not the pictures which causes trouble.

So far as a newsreel is concerned, I believe that many of the current war pictures will pass the Irish censor, provided care is taken to exclude those which the Irish may classify as propaganda: for example, I doubt that the Irish film censor would pass scenes of Allied troops being received with pleasure by the natives of Italy. Also it would be necessary to cut out 'horror scenes', such as of Axis dead and the like. Plain, objective battle scenes should pass the censor. It must be remembered that Irish film censorship is primarily concerned with excluding material which might cause disturbance in an Irish cinema.

With regard to the newsreel commentary: for Éire it should be written and spoken in an entirely objective and unemotional way. The Irish object to having English forces called 'our boys', Axis forces called 'the enemy' and so on. At first it might be necessary to avoid stressing which side is which. (The public in the cinemas will know anyway.)

If it were decided to have a newsreel service to Éire the following points might be considered:

1. Avoid pictures which could be criticised in Éire as 'un-neutral'
2. Stress American, Canadian and Australian participation and play down British participation (at first)
3. Realise that the Éire censor will be less sensitive about Pacific War scenes
4. Do not use any long scenes with United Nations personalities: Churchill would be regularly cut, Roosevelt sometimes
5. Remember that the British flag has regularly been cut in Éire and the Irish Free State (the American flag has never, so far as I know, been cut)
6. National anthems of belligerents will be cut
7. Use an entirely objective commentary – probably the less spoken the better
8. Have a speaker who at least will never mispronounce an Irish name or place

The newsreel companies, working together on some kind of a pool arrangement or with a single reel distributed by the several companies in Éire, could make a special newsreel for Éire pay expenses, I believe. This is probably on the condition that the small amount of raw film stock needed does not come out of their present quota. It would seem that it might be worthwhile for the government to make provision for the film stock needed to serve Éire with a newsreel.

7 September 1943

From John Betjeman of the Ministry of Information's film division, London

Dear Mr Quigley

Many thanks indeed for your most useful note on the newsreels for Éire. The advice in it is sound, practical and just what I want. I will let you know if anything transpires.

> *is mise*
> *le meas mór*
> John Betjeman

The Shelbourne Hotel, Dublin, 20 September 1943

Dear Governor

This will cover the week of September 13 to 18. On Monday and Tuesday of that week I was in London; I returned to Dublin on Wednesday.

In London last Monday I had a visit with John Hicks, foreign manager of Paramount, who, as you know, is making his first trip from New York since the start of the war. I saw Hicks with David Rose, Paramount managing director in England. Hicks and Rose plan to come over to inspect their Dublin branch office this coming weekend.

Before leaving London I also saw Ernest Simon of RKO Radio and Lacy Kastner, recently an executive in the Columbia Pictures foreign department but now representing the films division of the US Office of War Information in London. I told Kastner that I had suggested that some of the US newsreels made for neutral and other countries be submitted here for a censorship test. I first suggested that about June 1 and nothing had been received by the time I met Kastner. (You will see below that the first newsreels finally arrived.)

I had a very pleasant trip across from London. The train left Euston station at 8.30 and with breakfast and lunch taken on the train it was a short journey to Liverpool. The bus for the airport left at 1.45, three-quarters of an hour after the train arrived. After the usual customs inspections, the plane left. The Irish airlines, or Aer Lingus, as it is called, has a grand new Douglas plane just like the ones used on the US airlines. The trip across, in flying time, was hardly more than one hour. At Collinstown airport the immigration official marked my passport with a limitation of two months here instead of the three which I had expected.

The day after I arrived back in Dublin I attended a small luncheon given by Mrs Patrick Conway for Leo McCauley, the Irish Consul General in New York, who is currently on leave here.

When I got back to the hotel on Wednesday there was a message to call the American Consulate. Dan Terrell, the new press attaché and representative of the US Office of War Information, had called to let me know that the first of the American newsreels had arrived and could I arrange to have the film censor take a look at it. I told him I would talk to Dr Hayes the next morning.

Dr Hayes kindly consented to look at the American newsreel more or less informally. The screening was set for 3 pm on Thursday. That morning three more of the reels were received by Terrell from the US, so four were shown. They were the United Newsreels issues No. 61 to 64 inclusive. I am sure that the film censor found the reels very interesting. He indicated that he could pass almost all the material if there was no spoken commentary. This week it is likely that he will show the reels to some of the Irish officials.

Then I hope to take up the matter with the people in the film business here and try to arrange distribution of the reels – without sound, if necessary. When this is done the reels would be commercially imported, with duty as well as the censorship fees paid, and they would be formally submitted for censorship and application would be made for a licence for public exhibition. Terrell said that he has had no instructions about handling the United Newsreels so he is agreeable to anything I can work out with the film people.

Also I saw a couple of the film managers here – Mr Nash of Warners and Mr Livingstone of Twentieth Century-Fox. Had lunch with Mr O'Curry of the Catholic *Standard*, who has introduced several improvements in the column in his paper covering films and picture reviews since I have been here. But of course I do not agree with everything that paper says about pictures; in my opinion it sometimes takes contradictory viewpoints. Mr Sheehy, *Muintir na Tíre* (Rural Movement) was telling me about the plans that organisation has for using its mobile 16 mm truck for showings this winter. The group also has some 16 mm production ideas.

The weather was very cool, in contrast to London. Also it has been a bit on the moist side but yesterday was beautiful. I had my first (and doubtless only) sail of this season. O'Curry had me invited out by J. J. O'Leary of Cahill Press (which is publishing that Irish Cinema Handbook I have mentioned) and head of the Electrical Supply Board Tribunal to sail on his fine little cutter, *Windward*.

25 September 1943
Dear Governor
This will cover the period of September 20 to 25, a

somewhat hectic and most discouraging week from the point of view of film censorship.

I had thought that I had a pretty good understanding of the basis of Irish film censorship. During my four weeks in London I explained quite definitely the fundamental point of the censorship to the American company managers. Now I do not know where we stand.

In my letter of July 17 I reported on the position of Frank Aiken, Minister for the Coordination of Defensive Measures, that film censorship aims to eliminate anything that might cause a disturbance in a cinema. (Events of this week may indicate that I did not fully understand Aiken then.) Taking audience reaction as a starting point it was possible for me, through talks with people in all branches of the motion-picture industry both in Dublin and in a number of provincial cities and towns, to obtain a pretty good idea about what would or would not cause trouble in a cinema. An over-whelming majority in the business expressed the opinion that many of the things currently cut from films would cause no objectionable audience reaction at all. In fact, I was told everywhere that the only things that might cause difficulty would be violently pro-British pictures.

As you heard from the office in London, Twentieth Century-Fox's *A Yank in the RAF* passed the film censor here about six weeks ago. (Of course a number of cuts were ordered but these did not seriously interfere with the story.) After Mr Harley approved cutting the picture, that action was taken and the official film censor's certificate for public exhibition was issued. The picture opened last Friday, September 17, at the Savoy, the most important first-run Dublin cinema.

On Monday the film censor's office phoned the Twentieth Century-Fox branch and said the minister, Mr Aiken, wished to see the picture. A print was set up for the private showing at the censor's office on Wednesday morning, as requested. Late on Wednesday afternoon the censor's office informed Mr Livingstone, the Fox manager, by phone that the minister had ordered the certificate of *A Yank in the RAF* to be withdrawn as of Thursday night, permitting the first-week run at the Savoy to be ended.

This is the first action affecting a picture actually on the screen. Although a considerable time ago the Russian film *A Day in Soviet Russia* was advertised to open on Sunday and was ordered stopped on Saturday afternoon, *A Yank in the RAF* is the first American film whose certificate has been revoked in this fashion under the Emergency Powers Order. As I mentioned in my letter of June 26, any minister has the authority under the 1942 amendment of the Emergency Powers Order on pictures to issue a directive to the film censor before he has considered a film, while he is reviewing it or after it has been passed (as in this case).

Some 41,000 people saw the picture at the Savoy during its seven-day run and there was not the slightest suggestion of any unpleasantness. Almost 35,000 people had seen the film by the time the minister decided to revoke the certificate and have the picture taken off.

I have, of course, informed the American government authorities here about this matter, but in the name of the association I felt it necessary to attempt at least to obtain more information.

On Thursday morning I sent the following telegram to an Taoiseach, Éamon de Valera:

IT IS RESPECTFULLY SUGGESTED THAT YOU REVIEW PERSONALLY DECISION TAKEN TO REVIEW CERTIFICATE OF AMERICAN FILM A YANK IN THE RAF STOP THIS LOVE STORY WITH A 1940 WAR BACKGROUND HAS PLAYED TO 36,758 PERSONS AT SAVOY CINEMA DURING PAST SIX DAYS WITHOUT OCCASIONING SLIGHTEST INCIDENT OR CAUSING ANY OBJECTIONABLE AUDIENCE REACTION WHATSOEVER STOP UNDERSTAND CERTIFICATE IS BEING WITHDRAWN AS OF TONIGHT STOP I WOULD APPRECIATE AN OPPORTUNITY TO DISCUSS THIS MATTER WITH YOU OR YOUR REPRESENTATIVE

Later in the morning I received a telephone call from de Valera's private secretary, Miss O'Connell, telling me that she had brought the wire to de Valera's attention and that I should get in touch with Mr Aiken, Minister for the Coordination of Defensive Measures.

I called Aiken's office and was given an appointment to see him at 3.30 the next day, Friday.

Meanwhile the film trade here was becoming more and more concerned because it became known that Aiken had ordered a private screening at the censor's of the film *Crash Dive*. This picture was passed by the film censor about a month ago but, unlike *A Yank in the RAF*, it had not opened at a theatre. It was booked to follow the current film at the first-run Metropole in Dublin, however. A contract had been signed for a six-week run for *Crash Dive* as it is one of the best films of the year.

Aiken was pleasant but was not inclined to discuss the matter at any length. His position on *A Yank in the RAF* surprised me very much. He said that the film censor had eliminated any scene or remark on which an audience disturbance might arise. (That is the way we feel, also.) But Aiken went on to say that, while there is nothing in the film to which exception can be taken when in the cinema, when people went home and thought about the picture they did not like it and protested to him! I tried to point out that *A Yank in the RAF* is merely a Hollywood film of a routine type and is inconsequential so far as any propaganda is concerned. The elements of the film add up to the usual love story. There is not even any high motivation for the hero: he crossed the Atlantic to get $1,000 for flying a plane and he stays in England and joins the RAF merely to be near his girl, a dancer, played by Betty Grable. But you are familiar with the film – imagine it with about thirty cuts, including the entire sequence in Holland. I asked Aiken about the source of the complaints which had reached him. I tried to make sure that the people who had got in touch with him had actually seen the film. He assured me that the complaints came exclusively from Irish nationals. Evidently some consider the film pro-British. How that is possible is beyond me. The chief battle scenes in the film are Hollywood studio re-creations of Dunkirk, which was possibly the lowest point in Britain's history. Aiken said that in order to understand the feelings here we should think how we would feel if the Japanese had seized and occupied several of the western states (a reference to Partition, which seems to have its ramification in every Irish matter except the weather). Aiken continued by pointing out that the heart of the army, local defence force and so on is comprised of '1916 men' and that the government must not permit anything that would offend them.

I attempted to find out if objection was taken to the title

or to a word here or there or to some scene for those matters could be handled. It seems objection is taken to the spirit of the film, though I am convinced that there is not the slightest thing un-neutral in the spirit of *A Yank in the RAF.*

Aiken indicated that *Crash Dive* would be approved after a few additional cuts he had ordered, notably some bars of 'America My Country 'Tis of Thee' (similar to 'God Save the King').

I asked Aiken about the United Newsreels mentioned in my letter of September 20. He evidently had only a quick look at them but he did not seem to view them at all favourably. I had hoped that some of the scenes would be passed as they stand and practically everything else passed without the voice. The pictures are so interesting in themselves that I think they would be a good attraction with merely a few simple printed titles.

On Monday there was a meeting of the Kinematograph Renters Society (distributors) and I told the managers of the various American companies about my meetings in London in connection with Éire film problems.

Had a nice visit with Reverend T. Mulcahy SJ, editor of the *Irish Monthly* and some other Jesuit publications. Father Mulcahy is quite young, probably in his late thirties or early forties, and is very interested in films. I was glad to find that he did not take the attitude of some here that all films are to be criticised. In connection with the censorship of certain very Catholic films, Father Mulcahy expressed a possible viewpoint which I had not heard previously – he said the government here is anxious in every matter to avoid anything that might offend the Protestant minority. He said some of the latter might get the idea that the Catholic religion would be eventually forced on them should Catholic religious films and such be widely circulated. (This does not represent Father Mulcahy's own opinion but was only suggested as one possible angle.)

Basil Clancy, manager of the publication department of the Parkgate Press, Cahill & Co., showed me some proofs of the first edition of an *Irish Cinema Handbook,* which is now in press. The book will contain a lot of articles on the possible Irish use of films, chiefly for instruction, but it will also include what Clancy tells me is the best list ever of all Irish theatres and cinemas.

Fall is definitely here. The other day I thought I would get a few clothes-ration coupons to buy a pair of shoes designed for wet weather and some heavy socks but I was told at the Department of Supplies that one must be in the country six months before any clothes ration may be obtained. It was said that previously the regulation required a year's residence. In way of explanation I was told the country has only 10 per cent of its cotton needs and 30 per cent of its wool needs.

2 October 1943

Dear Governor

This will cover the week of September 27 to October 2.

Interest continued to centre around the situation created by the withdrawal of the Twentieth Century-Fox picture *A Yank in the RAF.* The matter was a main topic of conversation in the film circles here this week. On Tuesday there was a meeting of the general council of the Theatre and Cinema Association, the exhibitors organisation, to which I was invited as a guest. The exhibitors decided to send a delegation to see Frank Aiken, Minister for the Coordination of Defensive Measures, in order to explain how the revoking of a film censor's certificate affects their business and to inquire in general terms about the film censorship. The exhibitors selected the following to meet Aiken: Leonard Ging, Dublin second-runs; J. M. Stanley, Boyne cinemas; Mr Kirkham, subsequent runs and provincial houses; C. M. Conroy, manager of the Savoy Cinema, from which *A Yank in the RAF* was withdrawn; Gerald Ellis, chairman of the Theatre and Cinema Association and secretary of the Savoy company. That delegation saw the minister on Friday morning. Later I spoke to a couple of them and was told that the minister expressed sympathy with their position as exhibitors but pointed out that the cinema trade had suffered very little during this emergency period and was actually enjoying excellent business. It was also said that Aiken gave no indication of where the protests came from that resulted in the stopping of *A Yank in the RAF.* It was also asserted that the film censorship was as lenient as possible but that nothing would be permitted that might disrupt the unity of the nation.

Had another chat with Reverend Timothy Mulcahy SJ, editor of *The Irish Monthly, The Irish Jesuit Directory and Year Book* and *The Madonna,* a sodality publication, whom I mentioned meeting last week. Father Mulcahy was good enough to think over the subject of the film likes and dislikes of the Irish people and gave me the following list:

Likes

Musicals (except school and college co-educational productions)

Comedies (but not so much slapstick and more of the William Powell–Myrna Loy, Bob Hope variety)

Detective Stories

Wild West films

'Star Studded Spectacles'

Dislikes

Presentation of priests (indeed ministers of religion in general)

Fun during marriage ceremony

The list of 'likes' did not surprise me much for I have noted that Irish film tastes are very like American ones, but I was somewhat surprised that Father Mulcahy did not give a much longer list of 'dislikes'.

I met for the first time this week Liam O'Laoghaire (O'Leary), head of the Irish Film Society. I had a good talk with him and Edward Toner, another director of that organisation. The film society has presented during the past seven or eight winters a program of foreign films which have not been exhibited in this country, usually because of censorship or language difficulty. As would be expected, the society shows some Russian pictures; this has caused considerable criticism in the past. The programs of the society are for members only (subscription for nine shows, one guinea) and are not subject to the regular censorship. Last year one program had *49th Parallel* (called *Invaders* in the US), a British war feature. The society appears to be anxious, however, to avoid any controversy on that point (though they are content to risk church and other criticism on the Russian point) and no war topics are included this year. The organisation perhaps fears that it might be suppressed or have some other action taken against it.

Another organisation here which has motion-picture interests is the Cine Club. This group is especially interested in the technical point of view of the cameraman and director. I had a visit with Terence Sheehy, secretary of the Cine Club. It is too bad that in this small country there are so many groups with similar interests. One cinema organisation would be the right number, but there are at least half a dozen, and some are more or less at war with one another. Father Redmond took part of the membership away with him from the Cine Club when he founded the National Film Institute of Ireland; the *Muintir na Tire* (rural organisation) film unit also does not see eye to eye with the latter organisation. (I have pointed out that I cannot see why both 'National' and 'of Ireland' are in the title as they say the same thing.)

The *Irish Cinema Handbook* is now in press. Mr Clancy of the Parkgate Press showed me all the proofs yesterday. It will make an interesting book.

Leo McCauley, Irish Consul General for New York, took me to lunch at the University Club (headquarters of the Catholic University of Ireland nearly a hundred years ago, when it was headed by Cardinal Newman) to meet Lindsay Hogg, husband of the film actress Geraldine Fitzgerald.

There is nothing very new in connection with film censorship. The best story at the moment concerns RKO's *Bombardier.* Pat O'Brien, an officer-instructor, says, in the picture, to a class of bombardier recruits, 'There are three things a bombardier must remember − hit the target − hit the target − hit the target.' The film censor ordered that the last two 'hit the targets' be cut! Don't ask me why.

On Thursday I attended the final season outing of the Theatre and Cinema Golfing Association. It was a pleasant day and I met a number in the film industry and guests from many branches of activity.

You might tell your friends who are interested in horses and horse-racing that the Irish and English horseman must consider that the war is about over. The highest prices of all time were paid for yearlings at the annual sales at Ballsbridge. The average price in 1941 was 82 guineas, in 1942, 129 guineas and this year, 305 guineas. In 1926 the average price was 248 guineas, according to a piece in the *Irish Press*. One horse was sold for 2,800 guineas, which is a lot of money in any language, especially for a yearling which might never race.

I got a pair of shoes this week at a place where my father and I had riding boots made in 1939. It was lucky that I could find a pair in stock that fitted, for I was amazed to learn that it would take a year to have a pair made, so many orders are on hand.

Today is very beautiful. Fall is definitely in the air here, which is something one cannot say about summer at any time – in terms of summer as we know it in the US, that is.

5 October 1943
Dear Governor

This letter covers an aspect of the film situation here which, for obvious reasons, I could not discuss in a regular report.

As you have been informed, the Twentieth Century-Fox picture *A Yank in the RAF* was withdrawn by Minister Aiken after it had played seven days at the first-run Savoy cinema in Dublin. Yesterday an RKO 'This is America' two-reel short subject entitled *Army Chaplain* was ordered off the screen of the Regal Rooms Cinema. That subject was passed by the film censor on May 14 and during the past six weeks has played at five Dublin cinemas.

These two actions, as well as the general tone of the film censorship during the past two weeks, mean that the situation in this regard is just somewhat worse than when I first arrived in Éire in May. That would naturally call for an explanation. This morning I learned what appears to be the only possible basic reason and it makes the film censorship a part of something much larger.

An active man during the Troubles here was Emmett Dalton, who was with Michael Collins when he was killed. Dalton is now supervisor for Paramount, overseeing branch operations in the north of England, Scotland and Ireland. He has of course been disturbed about the new trend in film censorship on account of its potential effects on Paramount films. This morning Dalton took me to see General Mulcahy, one of the chief members of Fine Gael, Cosgrave's party, and currently a member of the Defence Commission and the Senate here.

After the film-censorship situation was explained to Mulcahy he gave the following explanation: the political purposes of Fianna Fail, de Valera's party, require that the country be kept in constant fear of some danger to neutrality. (Recent newspaper accounts of ministers' speeches warning of the continual presence of dangers to the country would appear to confirm this.) Mulcahy said that there was soon to be a sharply contested by-election in Tipperary and that there was the possibility of a general election in the spring.

The sharp current activities of the film censor and Mr Aiken are said to have a direct relation to these basic political purposes. Removal of these two American films will certainly have many hundreds of thousands of people throughout the country commenting on the action. Many are expected to see in the action indication of potential 'dangers' or 'threats' to this country which had to be avoided by sharp action by the political administration in power.

It was indicated that no improvement could be expected for at least several months, after which time political purposes will no longer require this use of film censorship. Mulcahy also indicated that he believed that it would not be good policy for Fine Gael to raise the matter of film censorship openly because, he pointed out, the government had all kinds of power now.

This position must seem strange. It may not be the true story but it is the best explanation of the sudden action in connection with the films that I have been able to get. The other two main rumours are that *A Yank in the RAF* was withdrawn as a result of either pressure from the German Legation or a threat from the IRA.

Neither of those rumours entirely satisfies me. (Nor does Aiken's reference to '1916 men' which I reported in a recent letter.) It does not seem likely that a protest from the German Legation, by itself, would result in stopping a picture at this late date in the war. The IRA theory is also not very convincing, although the current administration uses the IRA as an excuse for a lot of things. The IRA is a discredited group of people and it seems that the government would not pay too much attention to a protest from that quarter. Anyway, in the South the IRA is not believed to have any organisation except in the Curragh internment camp, where some 350 of an original 500 IRA men are locked up. (A number were recently released on their word to be 'good boys', and about another hundred, who have been convicted of criminal offences, are in a Dublin prison.)

Since the IRA was given as the excuse for certain film-censorship actions, however, I thought it would be best to find out whether that organisation had any policy towards motion pictures. I let it be known in a quarter that I thought would know some of the IRA that I was deeply interested in learning their views on films, on account of the censorship and because I wished to get the film views of all sections of the population.

My hint took effect and I had a very nice friendly talk with a man just released after three years and five months in the Curragh. He was more than a member on theoretical grounds, having had a part in the bombings in England in 1939. He claims that he finally decided that force was not the way, at least so far as the twenty-six counties are concerned, gave his word to avoid illegal activity and so was released. He told me that the IRA has no policy on films except that it would object to any picture deemed extremely pro-British. (The man had seen *A Yank in the RAF* and saw nothing in it but entertainment.) He said outside the Curragh the IRA had no organisation and each of the members was a law unto himself. He indicated that he believed the organisation was now, at least for the present, washed up, as we might express it. Part of the disillusionment resulted from the rank-and-file members learning that the leadership had been negotiating with the Nazis, notably the German agent (evidently the one mentioned in the newspapers by Minister for Justice Boland this summer) whom the IRA men knew as 'Herr Doktor'. From this data and indirect sources it appears that the IRA could not protest, even if it wished to, about these American films, and very likely there is nothing in *A Yank in the RAF* or *Army Chaplain* to which the IRA would have objected at any stage in its life.

All of which brings me back to the possible political reason for current film-censorship operations. The American film companies should expect especially harsh censorship treatment of their pictures at least for the next few months if this explanation is correct. The companies seem to have no choice but continuing as before or to discontinue sending new pictures into this country. If the latter action is considered it must be remembered that it is no good to threaten action; steps should be taken and further discussion had afterwards, if something of this sort is done.

10 October 1943

Dear Governor

This will cover the week of October 4 to 9.

On Monday afternoon there was a reception for Murray Silverstone, Twentieth Century-Fox vice-president in charge of foreign distribution; Francis Harley, managing director for the company in Europe; Sutton Dawes, sales director. Enclosed is a 'candid' photo from the *Times Pictorial*, a weekly combination revue and picture paper published by the *Irish Times*. It was at that reception that the motion-picture trade heard news that was even more mystifying than the withdrawal of *A Yank in the RAF* after its week at the Savoy. On Monday afternoon a two-reel short subject, *Army Chaplain*

(RKO 'This is America' series) was ordered stopped. This twenty-minute subject was passed by the Film Censor on May 14 and during the past six weeks had played at the following Dublin cinemas: the Metropole (two weeks), Theatre Royal (one week), Corinthian (one week), De Luxe (four days) and Regal Rooms (stopped after three days). During its various engagements, *Army Chaplain* must have been seen by about 70,000 people. It was of course booked into many other cinemas in Éire. I am not in a position to give any possible explanation why this short was stopped. It concerns, as you may recall, the army training at the special school at Harvard University of army chaplains of every denomination; it follows a Catholic chaplain into the battle area in the southwest Pacific.

I had a chat this week with Arthur Cox, a prominent Dublin solicitor said by some to be one of the best lawyers in the country. H. E. Guinness, managing director of Guinness & Mahon bank, suggested that I see Cox. I had an interesting talk with him about film censorship and explained that the recent actions perplexed me. Cox indicated that he understood how I felt because he said it was frequently hard for them to understand themselves. He also remarked that he saw no hope for improvement in the film situation. He pointed out that these were difficult days for this country and it had adopted an aloofness which is reflected in many things, including actions with respect to films.

Guinness took me to lunch at the Kildare Street Club, at one time an establishment much hated by the Irish as the headquarters of the 'Ascendancy'. Members of the club are still very Anglo-Irish but it would seem that it is not held in

the extreme disfavour that prevailed previously. The problem
is a difficult one though because, especially in Dublin, there
are almost two separate types of film audiences: the 'native
Irish' (divided into every branch of society from brilliant
intellectuals to the very ignorant, from the wealthy to the
very poor) and the Anglo-Irish, a big business class that is
generally either very comfortably off or rich. The Anglo-
Irishman in Dublin, even after generations, evidently does
not understand the native Irish at all. It is somewhat strange
because most of the native Irish have in their blood much
the same strains as the English but it seems that many or
most of the Anglo-Irish still consider themselves foreigners
here. That is perhaps somewhat natural, as the boys are
regularly educated in England or partly in England and partly
at Trinity College which looks to England; then they enter
businesses which have direct relationships with London. That
group looks on their circle in Dublin as an outpost of
London. I do not think it follows that any considerable group
of the Anglo-Irish are still anti-Irish or could be attacked as
unpatriotic to Éire but they simply have a different outlook.
It seems to me that, if it happens at all, it will be many years
before the Kildare Street Club type has the same viewpoint
as the native Irish. The Anglo-Irish, I suppose, would almost
all wish to see every film that is exhibited in London without
any further cuts by censorship.

Had an interesting visit with Frank Robbins, secretary
of the cinema branch of the Irish Transport and General
Workers Union (whom I mentioned meeting some time ago)
and two of the members of the union – one a projectionist
for twenty-five years and the other a despatch clerk in one
of the renters' offices. These men are naturally interested in

censorship of American films on account of the possible effect of this on the industry here.

Emmet Dalton has taken a keen interest in film censorship on account of its potentially serious effects on his company's business in Éire. Dalton is, of course, familiar with the Irish attitude and the personalities involved.

Peter O'Curry, editor of the Catholic *Standard,* took me out to Maynooth, the Catholic seminary for all the Irish dioceses, on Thursday afternoon. I was introduced to Dr Edward Kissane, the president, and Dr Patrick Brown by Father Timothy Shanley of St Matthew's parish in New York City. O'Curry is very familiar with Maynooth and many members of the faculty, having attended the seminary for a couple of years. Maynooth naturally exerts a tremendous influence on Irish life. All the parish priests and curates have their training there; the course lasts seven years. Most of the Irish bishops are graduates of Maynooth. In addition to the regular seven-year course there is a graduate school in several branches with courses lasting about three years. This graduate school was opened up this year for the first time to religious orders, who now find it almost impossible to send their picked men to foreign universities for final studies. I was glad to find that at Maynooth an interest is shown in motion pictures. Shows are held for the entire faculty and student body numbering perhaps 600 or more about once a month. Of course an effort is made to select outstanding motion pictures but the choice is not confined to religious or serious films. The aim, I believe, is to let the future priests and others there know something of the cinema, which is the chief form of recreation for the average man and woman almost everywhere in Éire.

The influence of Maynooth has extended to every parish in Ireland for the past century and a half. Also it is natural that in a country where over 90 per cent of the people are Catholic, some of the most learned Catholics – members of the faculty at Maynooth – would have a strong influence on governmental and educational circles generally.

The Irish Film Society opened its season on Saturday. One short subject shown was *Russian Salad*, which was rejected by the film-censor authorities. (I believe the picture had been passed by the film censor but was stopped before it had been shown in a cinema.) The film is composed exclusively of music, dancing and singing. There is not a single word of dialogue. The film could have been stopped solely because it was made in Russia. The Irish Film Society runs a small amateur school of film technique and has made several 16 mm silent pictures. I was shown several of these at the organisation's studio this week.

Had lunch one day with Helen Landreth, author of a book on Irish history published around 1937 called *Dear Dark Head*. Landreth has been engaged in work on Irish history for some time and hopes to spend the rest of her life doing research and writing books on Irish history during the period 1790 to 1805.

The cinemas and theatres continue to do good business in Dublin. With film censorship as it is, the theatre patrons are getting a much better variety of entertainment than the film fans. Almost every week several good plays are produced by competent companies here. On the other hand, it is sad to note how many fine films are not allowed in and how many others are cut so that their full entertainment quality is ruined.

20 October 1943

Dear Governor

This will cover the period of October 11 to 19, during which I visited Athlone, Ballina, Sligo, Bundoran and Dundalk.

A week ago Monday, the day before I left on the trip, Frank Robbins, secretary of the cinema branch of the Irish Transport and General Workers Union, took me to see Thomas Kennedy, a member of the Senate and the head of the union. We had an interesting talk with Kennedy and William O'Brien, his aide, on the background to film censorship and its potential relation to not only workers' entertainment but also employment. Any matter which may have an effect on employment is of course of interest to the union.

On Tuesday I arrived in Athlone, which is located almost at the geographical centre of Ireland, to find a big sheep fair in progress. The town was a mess. The railroad station was evidently constructed to be close to what was then a British military post and with no regard for the town. The walk seemed about a mile; perhaps it was less, for it was a wet morning. There are three cinemas in Athlone: a modern one, which seemed to be designed more for California than for Ireland, called the Ritz; an old converted hall on the river bank, the Savoy; and a converted barn, the Garden Vale.

John Duffy, manager of the Ritz, gave me some information on the types of films which are popular in Athlone. He has had a somewhat hectic career so far in the motion-picture business. He is a native of the North of Ireland and lost his job as chief projectionist in the 1935 troubles up there. In

Athlone and all the other towns of Éire (including Dublin, I understand) the cheapest seats – fourpence – are occupied in winter to a great extent by people who come into the cinema merely to get warm.

I called on Dr Chapman, the managing director of the *Westmeath Independent*, and Mr Glennon, the newspaper's editor. Both (as had others I met on this trip) criticised musical short films and also crime films which do not show that every criminal is punished or which tend to indicate that profit can be gained through a lie or even a petty theft. In the evening I had a long chat with Glennon. Also in Althone I saw Father Ferdinand OFM, who is very interested in films – he said he attends them to show some of the most conservative people that there is nothing wrong in them – and Canon Crowe who told me his brother is a pastor in Camarillo in California. Both Father Ferdinand and Canon Crowe indicated that they felt the government was handling the film censorship in a satisfactory manner. Of course, as priests they were concerned only with the moral censorship of the pictures. The anti-British feeling, however, seems more vital in the provincial towns than in Dublin. Perhaps that is especially true of places like Athlone, which were British garrison stations. The priests indicated that extremely pro-British pictures might not be well received but expressed the opinion that no adverse notice would be taken of films concerning either the war in the Pacific or American activities generally. On this trip it became clear to me that, from the average Irishman's point of view (not excluding the learned Irish) the war in the East seems as remote as if it were being fought on Mars. The people here seem to know virtually nothing about the Japanese. This fact makes the strict film censorship with regard to references to the war in the Pacific all the more mysterious.

On Wednesday afternoon I went to Ballina. The trains in Éire are comfortable enough, if very slow. In most cases there is only one train a day. The scenery in the middle of Éire, in contrast to areas near the coast, is dull and uninteresting. In Ballina I had a long visit on Wednesday evening with P. J. Mulligan, a prominent west of Ireland solicitor who operates cinemas in Galway and Ballina. His partner is Mrs Egan, wife of the head of one of the big bottling companies. Ballina's Estoria Cinema, which Egan designed, was the first built in Ireland especially for sound motion pictures, according to Mulligan. For a long time it was the only cinema offering sound in County Mayo. There is a peculiar film problem in Ballina in that, according to Mulligan and Egan, only a fraction of the population attends films and only a few hundred people are regular patrons of cinemas. This is somewhat strange, as the population is almost 6,000. I was told that the people spend their time playing cards and reading (and I suppose, as in most places in Ireland, a good percentage of the people spending a lot of time drinking). Mulligan, though a lawyer, could not explain the film-censorship position here. Many businesses have similar troubles.

On Thursday morning in Ballina I called on Frederick V. Devere, head of *Western People,* the largest provincial paper in Ireland. I was surprised to see that the newspaper is printed on a modern Chicago-built four-deck press capable of making 35,000 copies an hour. Of course now, with paper rationing, the paper uses four instead of sixteen pages and only needs one of the four decks of the press. Devere evidently is one of the deans of Irish journalism as many men, both on the editorial and printing sides, 'graduate' from his paper to jobs on the Dublin dailies. He personally said he likes most films and realizes the need even for the films he does not care for. He remarked that, as in a newspaper, it is necessary to please all tastes. At Devere's office I was introduced to John Clark, a local drug-newspaper store operator, who married in Chicago. It is quite surprising how frequently you meet in Éire people who have spent some time in the US and returned here, in many cases to take over management of a farm or a business that has been left to them.

I went on to Sligo on Thursday evening. There are two cinemas in Sligo – the Gaiety, operated by a local company, and the Savoy, which has just been sold by a local man to the Curran circuit, which has about ten cinemas in the North of Ireland. Curran himself was at the Savoy because it was the first week of operation of his first cinema in Éire territory (though he doubtless intends to expand his chain of theatres here). Curran, of course, is from Northern Ireland, as is his manager, Mr Bradley. Naturally neither could supply any information on film tastes in Sligo as they were preparing to try to learn them for themselves. We did, however, have a good chat about film problems in general. Curran knows that he is going to have all kinds of problems operating the cinema in Sligo because the films will have to be booked and handled entirely separately from his other cinemas in the North. (Those being in Northern Éire get the films from Belfast shipping offices and are not subject to additional censorship beyond what is done in London.) A picture might play on one side of the border months or years before playing on the other. It was in one of Mr Curran's cinemas that some time ago the IRA head came in with some of his gunmen and made a speech to the audience. I was interested to learn that the audience was not upset at the sudden interruption and sat quietly through the speech, even applauding McEteer, or whatever his name was, when the speech was over, perhaps in appreciation of the singular and unexpected entertainment.

On Friday morning I saw Kenneth Paton, manager of the Gaiety Cinema, and I later had lunch with him. I called to see the bishop, Dr Doorly, but was sorry to learn that he had not yet returned from the bishops' meeting at Maynooth College. I did, however, have a long chat with Father Thomas Hanley, one of the priests attached to Sligo Cathedral. Father Hanley said the Sligo audiences liked high-class musical films, of the Jeanette McDonald–Nelson Eddy type. He also pointed out that Irish audiences have not been trained to appreciate Walt Disney films. They do not care for the fantasies in colour. They want pictures that are more real (but not pictures that require thought). Father Hanley also discussed the peculiar difficulties this country has in administering its censorship: its desire to keep friends with everyone, its old hatred for England and the fact that it is a new nation and therefore lacks experience in these matters. Father Hanley said that American business interests should try to understand these difficulties and not be impatient. He also talked, as several other people have to me, about the desire of many in Éire to be somehow linked with the United States. In the minds of many Irishmen the 700 years of troubled history with England overbalances the geographical considerations. It would seem that Éire would like to be a 'good neighbour' with England but has no wish to be on any intimate terms with her. This feeling is also marked in the film business. Certain Irish nationals resent the present set-up, under which matters are referred to London by the Dublin film offices; these people would much prefer to have them decided by New York. Perhaps that is a general feeling.

In Sligo I also saw Martin Roddy, a member of the Dáil and editor of the *Sligo Champion* and another weekly which is circulated in Donegal and in Northern Ireland. Roddy pointed out that Sligo is a very musical town: it has one music that has been in existence for a hundred years. He said that good musicals would always be a success there. He made no comments on the film censorship other than to indicate that he feels the film censor is doing a good job. At lunch with Paton I was somewhat surprised to learn that there are two classes of film audiences in Sligo – Catholic and Protestant – and there are such things as all-Catholic and all-Protestant business concerns. After lunch Paton showed me around the town, a chief characteristic of which is a river which divides it. The salmon runs here earlier than anywhere in the British Isles. This brings a fortune to the man who owns the rights.

The run along the coast by bus on Friday afternoon (the Ballina–Sligo trip was also by bus) was quite beautiful, even though it was a dull and rainy day. The seascape at Bundoran is the most beautiful I have ever seen. In parts it reminded me of the coast at Del Monte, California. From the station in Bundoran I had to walk the mile to the Great Northern hotel but a native took my bag in a tiny donkey cart – one uses all kinds of transportation these days in Éire. I had expected the hotel to be very crowded but the season had ended a week or so before and there were only about half a dozen guests. I was invited to join the table of a Northern Ireland businessman named Dickson who had with him a son on leave and two British engineers enjoying their first holiday in several years. It was a pleasant weekend.

My main purpose in going to Bundoran was to see Father Connolly, head of the St Joseph's Orphanage there and operator of the resort's only cinema. I had a good visit with Father Connolly and Father Little, one of the curates of the parish, who lives at the orphanage and takes a keen interest in the cinema. The story is rather interesting. A boys' and a girls' orphanage were set up in Bundoran in 1909 with money left by the sole survivor of a family which emigrated to the US and made a lot of money in New England. An endowment of £50,000 was invested in Great Northern and Great Southern Railway stocks, which were considered absolutely safe. The orphanages had an adequate income for some years but in more recent times the railways stopped or almost stopped paying anything. Donegal is a poor area and the people of Bundoran and surrounding towns could never raise the money. Father Connolly, who has been at the orphanage for eighteen years, fortunately seems to be a good business-man. He started a laundry to raise some money. This has been, I would guess, quite successful but I would think his major source of revenue is the cinema which he took over four or five years ago. It had been a failure; he spent quite a sum fixing it up and has made money on it ever since. The problem is not easy, for Bundoran has only a tiny population, perhaps 1,400 in the off-season (there are crowds from July to September). Father Connolly is very worried at the moment, though, because on August 1 the government passed a law making all charitable entertainments subject to the entertainment tax (which is about 25 per cent) if the expenses exceed 30 per cent. As the orphanage owns the cinema, there has previously been no tax. Father Connolly hopes that he can keep expenses down to 30 per cent, especially in the off-season, but the matter has also been referred to the bishops, who might ask the government for relief for this and perhaps a dozen similar cases. For it is one thing to run a dance or similar charity event and keep expenses below 30 per cent but it is something else to run a business and keep all costs below 30 per cent. The summer audiences and the townspeople like fairly sophisticated pictures at Bundoran; the people who come in from the country like more action: westerns and gangster pictures. The weather at Bundoran was perfect; this was rather unusual, for it frequently rains in the west of Ireland.

The trip across Ireland from Bundoran to Dundalk should really be made the theme of a musical motion picture (and a comedy at that). The train route touches Northern Ireland at several places. I had expected that passengers originating in Éire and going through to destinations in Éire would be in a train car that would go right through. (Baggage could be put in a sealed van, which would save some bother.) The train left Bundoran shortly after twelve thirty and in a few minutes we were in Ballyshannon. There the Éire customs did their inspecting. After a wait, we were off again (slowly) to Belleek, where the Northern Ireland customs inspected the baggage. Then the train seems to wiggle back and forth along the border (which one does not notice at all). In Pettigoe there was no customs inspection. I was told that Pettigoe is one of the strangest places – half in Northern

Ireland and half in Éire. At night one half is completely blacked out and the other is ablaze with lights. (That place should be a scene for a play or part of a film.) At Kesh there was another Northern Ireland customs inspection. (I realize that that works out unevenly. To match up one would have expected an Éire customs to precede the Northern Ireland one, but this did not occur.) Also at Kesh there was an inspection of identity cards by a Royal Ulster Constabulary sergeant in a fine uniform complete with a Wild West-style revolver on the outside. A bit further on, at Bundoran Junction, we had to get off the train. I was told by the conductor that there was no point in waiting there because there was nothing to be seen (it was merely a railway crossing). I was told to take a train to the next town, which I did – that was Enniskillen in County Fermanagh. I had about three-quarters of an hour to kill so I just walked down the main street. The town looked just like many others I have seen in Ireland, except that one missed the English-Irish nameplates of streets and other signs and the quaint Gaelic script. Notable features included the fact that there were a few military uniforms and of course more military vehicles than one sees on the streets in Éire; there were also a large number of police, patrolling in twos. Shortly after boarding the train at Enniskillen again, we came to New-townbutler, I think the name was, and there was another Northern Ireland customs inspection and an inspection of identity cards. This time, however, the inspection was done by a military-police fellow who was dressed in despatch rider's garb with helmet, goggles and all. Quite a contrast from the RUC uniform on the way in. A little further on, after going even slower than before, the train reached Clones, where there was another inspection by the Irish customs and the sealed luggage van could not be opened. Éire takes no note of anything but customs between the parts of Éire. Northern Éire in addition to customs takes a look at identity cards but no records are made.

It has certainly taken a lot of space to describe the trip but I assure you that it was quite a long train ride for such a short distance. I arrived in Dundalk at about 7pm and called to see Father J. F. Stokes. Father Stokes is administrator of the parish there for the Cardinal. Also he is the chief priest–cinema operator in Éire – perhaps in the world. He has what is said to be the best cinema in the town, the Magnet. Father Stokes told me that the Cardinal does not altogether approve of a priest operating a cinema. Father Stokes has however pointed out that such an operation can tend to elevate film standards. I do not know whether that argument convinces Cardinal MacRory (or Father Stokes himself). I should guess the reason why Father Stokes is in the cinema business is the same one that motivated Father Connolly to run the cinema in Bundoran, i.e. money, but many more people object to Father Stokes's operation than do to Father Connolly's. The Dundalk parish has its regular sources of income, whereas the orphanage lost its source of income, and so on. Some people claim that there is no more reason for priests in Éire to operate cinemas in ordinary towns, like Dundalk, than, say, run public houses or any other business which will make money. I believe that some time ago I mentioned J. M. Stanley's views on this matter. Of course he is an interested party as he owns one of the cinemas in Dundalk, which he freely states cannot keep up with the competition offered by Father Stokes's cinema, which is run by volunteers and has very low expenses. I should not be surprised if such activities as Father Stokes's (despite his fine motives) are contributing to the small but apparent anti-clerical tendencies in Éire. Father Stokes personally is a charming man. He seems to know a good deal about motion pictures. (For example in Dublin he had seen the film *A Yank in the RAF* and could not understand why it was stopped.) It is also clear that he does not devote any great part of his time to the cinema as he runs a big cathedral church in Dundalk, has just opened a very large residence and probably is one of the Cardinal's advisers. I was sorry that I arrived in Dundalk at an inconvenient time. I had only rather brief visits with Father Stokes on Monday night and Tuesday morning as the Cardinal had arrived there and conferences were scheduled.

I called to see the editor of the chief paper in Dundalk but he was not in. I had a little talk with Mr Boyle of the *Dundalk Examiner*: the editor of that paper was also away. Boyle pointed out that it is sometimes very hard to know what people will want in entertainment as frequently the best drama and music performances in Dundalk are not well supported and mediocre ones are packed.

On Friday afternoon I have been asked to talk to the English group of Trinity College, Dublin. I plan to talk about the Story Film and its relation to the novel and the play. Early in November I am to make a speech to the Writers' Guild of the Writers, Actors, Artists and Musicians Association.

London, 13 November 1943

Dear Governor

This will cover the week of November 7 to 13. I travelled from London to Dublin on the afternoon of November 12.

Last Sunday I had dinner at the home of Peter O'Curry, editor of the *Standard* in Ballybrack, a Dublin suburb. Father Canesa, a Spanish Jesuit, was also present. We had an interesting discussion about certain points raised in connection with the ban on the RKO short *Army Chaplain*; I have not previously mentioned this ban in my letters. The conclusion was that not only was the film fit and proper but the same obligation rests on any priest anywhere at any time to minister to a dying man in the light of the man's views. On Sunday evening the O'Currys took me to a supper at the home of Senator and Mrs Tierney, who live near them. Senator Tierney is a professor of Greek in the National University Dublin and is vice-chairman of the Senate. Mrs Tierney is a daughter of Owen MacNeill and a niece of James MacNeill, both formerly prominent in Irish politics. Others at the Tierneys' were Dr Theo Dillon, a brother of the TD James Dillon and also a great (and very interesting) talker; Professor Delargy, an expert in Irish folklore, and Mr Fitzgibbon, architect of Dublin Corporation. It was quite an evening of conversation, which is a fine art in Irish intellectual circles. Dr Dillon told some extremely funny stories but, as one would expect, most of the conversation was on politics and education. There is little satisfaction about either in Éire.

On Tuesday I had a nice visit with the Papal Nuncio, Archbishop Pascal Robinson, at the nunciature in Phoenix Park. (That was the second secretary's place under British rule; the American Legation being the first secretary's and the home of the president being the governor's place.)

I told His Excellency about the action taken on the film *Army Chaplain*. He explained that doubtless someone considered that the picture might give scandal in Éire. He added that they were 'narrow' and 'old-fashioned'. I also told him about the film *The Eternal Gift*, which has also been banned for public or private exhibition in Éire even though it has a foreword by the Archbishop of Chicago and a commentary by Monsignor Sheen and was produced by the Servite Fathers. I also mentioned the French film on the Passion. He indicated that he would not care to see such a picture himself but would not object to others seeing it. I do not think that there is much that the Papal Nuncio feels he can do in this matter. I did learn later, however, that he said he was very surprised to be told about these films of a religious nature which are not allowed to be shown in Éire. A further question arises from the fact that these films have been stopped, it is believed, directly by the Archbishop of Dublin, Dr McQuaid. He, however, has jurisdiction only over his own diocese, and other bishops in Ireland resent the fact that his influence with the film censor achieves control of films in their dioceses. One is frequently told the story in Ireland about there being not 'twenty-six bishops there but twenty-six popes'.

Also in the early part of the week I met Mr Ryan, the editor of the *Irish Catholic*, and Mr Fogarty, its business manager. The *Irish Catholic* is a weekly paper which carries more detailed and minor religious news and fewer items of political and national importance than the *Standard*, which has about three times its circulation. The *Irish Catholic* has been giving attention to films for a long time. Its basic aims, according to the editor, are 'for clear pictures'. The matter is somewhat confused in my mind and possibly among the management of the paper because Fogarty told me he objected to the bathing-beauty scenes in the Andy Hardy films! I am afraid that he must belong to the school in Ireland which insists (in many, or rather most, places) that men and women swim in different parts of the beach. The *Irish Catholic* likewise has a great belief in the neutrality of Ireland without, it would seem to me, having any great understanding of the actual situation.

On Tuesday afternoon I had a very pleasant chat with Professor Delargy, who has received some assistance from the Rockefeller Institute in his work of recording Irish folklore and native storytellers. Among many other topics we discussed the possible uses of motion pictures to record the sound of these stories and pictures of the men and women in the native, original surroundings by means of a mobile unit.

On Wednesday afternoon I had an interview with de Valera. It was especially nice of him to spare the time then because the Dáil was in session and two budgets in which he is directly concerned – those of the Department of the Taoiseach and the Department of External Affairs – were up. I saw him in his office in Leinster House, where the Dáil meets, and not in his regular place in government Buildings. I thought that no useful purpose could be served by discussing censorship of the films, so instead I asked him if he had any comments on American pictures he wished me to take back to the producers.

De Valera then spoke, as he did when I saw him on about

the first of June, on his belief in the motion picture as the greatest force for education. (He prefaced his remarks by the statement, which is unfortunately all too true, that he does not see many films and knows little about them.) He said that he does not believe, as some do, that all films should be educational but he thinks there should be a mixture of education and entertainment. He mentioned a film on the growth of a fern which was shown recently in Galway. (This was doubtless called to his attention by his daughter, who is professor of biology at Galway University.)

After the war, de Valera continued, he believes that the motion pictures will be a great force for peace. He said that he thought that after the last war they had served a good purpose by showing people what the war was like. He indicated that he believed they had an even greater mission of the kind coming. He said he thinks, after the present war, the Irish people should see such films so they will know what the war is like.

He made references to the problem of partition: he said he hoped the films would make for peace after the war. He indicated in general terms that sometimes force may be necessary and that wars will probably always come, but at less frequent intervals, it is hoped. He spoke of the evils done by certain leaders who are in power for only ten or fifteen years but the effects of whose actions cause troubles for generations who had no part in the original issue at all – another reference to Partition.

De Valera said that, as Churchill had stated, he thought there would be great loss of life in the next year of the war. He asked me to tell his friends in America that he was doing the best he could and thanking God every day that Éire has been spared devastation in this war.

On Thursday morning I called on Mr Gray, the US Minister. Gray believes that the film companies should take a firm stand on the matter of Irish censorship of pictures. He indicated that unless firmness is shown he will be able to do nothing further on the question, except, of course, if requested from Washington.

On Thursday the representatives of the film companies in Dublin gave a little lunch for me at the Gresham. It was very pleasant. They seem to feel that I had accomplished something, especially in the matter of goodwill for the picture business there, despite the fact, which I freely stated, that my business in connection with film censorship was largely a failure. The censorship is definitely as bad as or worse than ever and the tightening up about the latter part of September is extremely difficult to understand.

I arrived in London last night at about 10.15 pm. This morning I went to the American Embassy with a form in connection with my transportation. Miss Maitland, Mr Allport's secretary, had made the preliminary arrangements. While nothing definite was said I got the impression that I would be getting a boat quite soon and should have no difficulty reaching New York by December 1, as requested in your cable.

16 November 1943

Dear Rebel

On this trip I crossed over to Éire on September 15 and returned to London on the evening of November 12. (I was landed on the condition that I remain there not later than November 15. As I wrote through the association I had expected to be given three months, as on the first trip but I was limited to two.)

I am very glad to report that everything went well. However the situation took a peculiar turn and I would not have been very surprised had I been asked to leave Éire, and I feel pretty sure any request for an extension of my stay beyond November 15 would not have been well received.

This does not concern my cover which, I believe, is firmly established in all quarters in Éire. In fact I feel that the natural suspicion was entirely removed as time went on, but my cover activity became annoying or objectionable to the Irish authorities and consequently even more delicate. The fundamental reason for this is not very clear. In the latter part of September the Irish censorship authorities decided to tighten up on the film censorship. Why, I do not know. Perhaps one reason was they wanted to make sure they were not relaxing under pressure of the trend of the war, so in quite typical Irish fashion they determined to lean over backwards.

The result of this, as it affected me, was that my routine work of cover visiting the film censor's office was more or less ruled out. My presence embarrassed him because he probably blamed some of the increased pressure from his superiors on me. It might have been asserted that he was yielding to the quiet pressure on the film censorship. The development did not please me but there was nothing I could do about it. The film censor's office had previously served as a fair source of good information and a routine business cover and I had previously spent three or four mornings a week there. It gave me the appearance of having a regular activity.

Moreover, since the Irish authorities had decided to

tighten up on the film censorship instead of relax it (or at the very least keep it the same) and I was supposed to be representing the American producers, I had to do what I could. Since the matter was then out of the hands of the film censor, I had to apply pressure on the responsible party, Frank Aiken, Minister for the Coordination of Defensive Measures. I saw the minister and then encouraged exhibitors, Fine Gael and labour interests to take up the matter of film censorship with him, so it was not surprising that my name became unpopular with Aiken. The secretary of the cinema union told me that when the labour delegation saw Aiken about film censorship (as a potential threat to their jobs) and my name came up in the conversation, 'Mr Aiken saw red.' From another source I learned that in the same interview, when one of the labour men referred to the alleged belief that the German minister had some influence in the matter of film censorship, Aiken exclaimed with considerable vigor, 'I do not care any more for the German minister than I do for Martin . . .'

Contacts first established in the spring were developed and new ones were made. My two trips into the country were also very satisfactory.

My cover is established 100 per cent with the American minister. An embarrassing situation would arise should he learn of my work. While I do not know his motives, I now agree with his judgment that there should be no secret-intelligence use of the legation there: I was informed that its wires are tapped, etc.

The association office here has started arrangements for my transportation with the American Embassy. Yesterday I purchased a $150 ticket on United States lines and expect to learn tomorrow where and when and to what port to go.

My health continues excellent though I have lost a little weight.

    With best wishes,
    Yours sincerely,
    Martin

('Rebel' was the code name for Francis P. Miller.)

CODA

When I returned from Ireland, reporting in December 1943 to OSS headquarters in Washington, DC, it was decided that I should be sent back to Éire some time in 1944 using the same cover – as a representative of the Motion Picture Producers & Distributors of America. In order to broaden my contacts in Ireland I was authorized to write a short book, which, after review by R. Carter Nicholas, OSS Irish Desk Head, and General William J. Donovan, OSS Director, was published under the title *Great Gaels – Ireland at Peace in a World at War*.

Approximately a hundred copies of the book were mailed to people I had met in Éire, but only a few ever got delivered. Presumably a big pile of the copies accumulated in the postal censor office in Dublin and were eventually destroyed.

Changing conditions in the war, including the successful Allied invasion of Normandy and increasing contact with Irish officials by overt OSS representatives, made it unnecessary to send me back to Éire under cover (or send any other OSS officials under commercial cover), so I was transferred, with the approval of Whitney Shepardson, head of the OSS strategic intelligence branch, to the Italian section. When the liberation of Rome was accomplished, I was to go there and collect strategic intelligence at the Vatican and at the various headquarters of Catholic religious organisations.

Before leaving Washington to go to Rome (where I lived and worked apart from the OSS organisation), I received a special order directly from General Donovan: 'Be alert at the appropriate time to find a way to open up communications looking to the surrender of Japan.' That I accomplished in the spring of 1945, two months before the atom bombs were dropped on Hiroshima and Nagasaki. That story is told in my book *Peace Without Hiroshima – Secret Action at the Vatican in the Spring of 1945*.

I have had no contact or connection with the US intelligence community since shortly after the end of World War II. My OSS service ended on 17 August 1945. Decades after the end of that war, Congress, in its wisdom, decided that OSS secret intelligence agents who had served overseas under cover should be awarded military status retroactively. So it was that, almost half a century after the end of hostilities, I was discharged from the US Army on November 6, 1990. The discharge, perhaps understandably, was without a rank.

And so this US spy in Ireland came in from the cold at last.

Appendix

An Espionage Primer

On my return to the United States from my stay in Éire, my OSS superiors at headquarters in Washington, DC, asked me to prepare notes on commercial cover and techniques of reporting that might be useful in the training of future spies. At that time no one knew how long the war – in Europe against the Germans and in the Pacific against the Japanese – might last. The longer the armed conflict lasted, the greater the need would be for the recruitment and training of intelligence officers.

The following is the text of my notes written early in 1944:

Notes on Cover

A cover must be natural and must be adequate.

If possible, the cover should fit perfectly with the individual's background and experience. At the very least the cover should be one which the individual can easily assume and carry on with the minimum chance of detection from enemies or friends.

To be adequate, a cover must make it practical for the individual to travel to his destination, freely circulate there, be able to meet and talk with all the people he wishes to see and have contact with his means of communication.

It must be recognized that there is no such thing as a perfect cover. Some covers sacrifice ease of communications for security; others are weak in security but satisfactory for an operation which does not extend over a considerable period of time. Every cover will not be equally strong in all respects, but the cover should be natural and adequate, at least for the purposes in view. The limitations of a particular cover should be understood in advance. Such knowledge can save a lot of difficulty later on.

In addition to the background, experience and temperament of the individual concerned, there are a number of external facts which affect the cover, including the country involved and its relation to other nations, activities of those who may aim to expose a cover, the length of time required for the operation and the security needed.

Assuming selection of an adequate and natural cover for the task in mind, there are several factors which assist in making the cover effective.

First of all, the cover must be 'lived' before, during, and after the operation.

Secondly, at all times, and especially during activity in the field, the cover must be worked at. It is not sufficient for the individual to claim that he is engaged in a particular job. He must make it clear to all interested parties that he is actually doing that job and is fully qualified for it. In conversations with people abroad, both inside and outside the area of his cover, the individual should always keep the cover activity well known in the minds of the other parties.

At times this may require the individual to appear to be uninterested in something (even though it is of primary importance) because it is outside the cover. On the other hand, the individual must be very interested in problems of his cover activity when with or observed by others, although the cover may have no real personal attraction.

Thirdly, the cover should be positively impressed upon people in a position to do special harm or special good. If the cover is natural and adequate, there is still a basic danger that the cover may not be made known in every necessary quarter. People are suspicious, especially in troubled times and in countries with a long history of strife. If the people do not know what the explanation of the individual's presence and activity is, they will think up one for themselves. They might guess correctly if allowed to do so or they might guess something equally upsetting.

Provided it is consistent with movements in the cover, steps should be taken at the first opportunity to make the cover activity and the reasons for it and the individual's presence known to people who might otherwise cause trouble, i.e. high police or government officials and local people in the same type of business as the cover. If these people have no explanation they may seize on one. If the individual properly puts over his cover with these people, any suspicion would first have to displace the impression previously created. Otherwise it would grow on open ground. For example, should a routine investigation be ordered, it probably would be dropped quickly after a cursory check if the individual is found to have made known to prominent persons what he is supposed to be doing. Should the few necessary important persons be convinced, the many others will probably cause no trouble.

The best cover is one that does not limit the individual in any way. He should be free to travel where and when he desires in the particular country. It should be fitting and proper for him to speak to anyone and everyone he wishes, especially people who influence local opinion and actions. The cover should fully justify his living, entertainment and business expenses. Also, if possible the cover should be of a character which tends to draw others out and one in which many diverse people may be interested. But above all, the cover should be suitable to the type of operation contemplated.

Notes on Information

General principles of good journalism serve as a fundamental guide to standards for obtaining and reporting strategic and other information.

Attention must be given to: who, what, where, when, why and how. A sharp distinction must be made between facts and opinions and the reporter's personal interpretation of the situation. Depending on the particular matter, all three may be important. At times, reporting of trends, opinions and ideas may be as valuable as reporting physical facts. Also, the reporter's personal judgement may be useful. It must be remembered, however, that although the reporter has the advantage of being on the spot, generally he will not have available all the information which the office will have on the situation. The office has the advantage of being able to weigh information from a number of sources and is in a better position to take a long view of a situation.

In reporting facts or trends and opinions, objectivity must be the goal. Obviously it is necessary to strive to reach a representative cross-section of local life, in the social, political, and intellectual spheres and in the geographical divisions of the country.

Any report, no matter how complete, involves selection and emphasis of details. Here the reporter must observe strict caution. Facts and opinions must be organised and briefly set down but they must not be marshalled into any preconceived or evolved personal idea of what the facts and attitudes of the situation should be. In this work the reporter is not trying to prove a case, as a lawyer at a trial. The reporter must make sure that his own views do not distort the picture which he is relaying to the office.

In a word, a reporter should be informed, accurate and objective.

Reporting facts is simpler than reporting ideas, trends and opinions, but it is a good idea to bear in mind that ideas, aims and movements precede and inspire actions of all kinds. The opinions which become dominant today result in tomorrow's actions.

In reporting facts, it is above all essential to be accurate. Nothing should be stated as a fact which may be only probably or possibly true. Generalisations are usually dangerous. No human is all-wise. Facts should be stated as they are known. If the facts, or alleged facts, are based on some authority, that source should be given. If the 'facts' may or may not be true, that should be indicated clearly.

In connection with reporting attitudes and opinions, it is important to realise that the idea cannot be divorced from the person or group having it. In other words, it is necessary to make known not only the particular attitude or opinion but also who holds that view. In a nation or a smaller community, everyone has ideas and opinions but the attitudes of all types of people do not have the same potential effects. Of special importance, of course, are the attitudes and opinions of those who can or do influence public opinion and actions of every kind in the particular community or country.

There follow a number of useful hints in connection with the process of obtaining information.

First of all, the reporter must have or develop an interest in the various subjects and individuals under consideration.

It is necessary to be able to discuss matters and views intelligently rather than merely to ask questions. In many cases a direct question will not produce an answer. In other cases the answer to a direct question will be so carefully delivered that parts of the truth are concealed and the proper emphasis is altered.

One way of having an opinion or discussion of a situation more fully developed is to adopt a puzzled or slightly opposed attitude to that of the person or persons being interviewed. This may encourage a full and detailed explanation. On the other hand, a definite, outspoken opposition to the views of the other party will regularly lead nowhere so far as obtaining useful information is concerned. That also has the danger of resulting in the reporter concentrating on his own opinions and becoming involved in controversies or arguments.

The opposition, official or merely personal and unorganised, is frequently a good source of information. Of course, caution is necessary in making use of the opposition in any matter because its aims will colour what is said and done.

But in general, the opposition, being on the outside of any situation, has less to lose by being frank. The party in power, the leading group or the dominant movement or individual usually has published or proclaimed all they wish known and are particularly on guard to conceal what is not favourable to their position. On the other hand, the opposition is ready, or over-ready, to make known the faults of the other side in an official, business, or private matter. Furthermore, being in the minority – at least in influence – the opposition is usually eager to expound its views and win over others to its opinions.

It is always essential for a reporter to remember that people have a habit of frequently saying what they think the other fellow wants to hear. Also, people do not always speak the truth.

The quest for information abroad has extra difficulties. The reporter must guard against distorting people and situations by seeing them with the eyes of a typical American tourist instead of in the context of the realities of the matter.

The reporter should realise that there are not entirely simple explanations of complex situations – and almost every foreign problem or situation is complex. The reporter should avoid general and sweeping conclusions. He must also keep in mind that it is almost certain that he does not know all the facts and it is possible that the contrary of his private opinion may be true because unknown or unappreciated forces are at work. The reporter must avoid snap judgements and continually try to make sure that he has uncovered every pertinent fact and keeps acquainted with all new facts as they develop in every situation.

One method that may be useful in learning more about a

situation is to put oneself mentally in the other fellow's place. That might make both the other fellow and the situation more understandable. The attitudes of many foreign nations and groups are difficult for us to understand at all unless we consider how we would feel and act in similar circumstances.

Naturally this does not mean that the reporter should believe the other fellow is right. All of that is outside the province of the reporter. While his own conclusions may be valuable, his prime duty is reporting, i.e. finding information that is representative of the situation and passing it on to the office without colouring it in any way. The reporter must strive continually to keep his personal views distinct from his reports of facts, opinions and attitudes.

Without intelligent, fair and objective reporting, the office is virtually powerless. Reporting fulfills a prime function of the entire operation.

INDEX

Aiken, Frank, 21, 23, 70, 77, 105, 127, 136, 137-9, 150, 163, 169, 171-3, 175, 178, 180, 202
Allport, Fay, 59, 116, 158, 159, 202

Baker, A. D., 155
Barfield, Norman, 90
Beale, Tom, 109, 111
Beddington, Jack, 160, 161, 163
Betjeman, John, 155, 160-1, 163, 166
Blenner-Hassett, Roland, 16-17
Boland, Gerald, 21, 127, 150, 182
Bowden, George K., 50
Brian, Colonel Dan, 64
Brown, Dr Patrick, 185
Brown, J. Walton, 160, 162
Browne, Bishop Michael, 129-30
Bryan, Dan, 21
Burnup, Hope Williams, 58-9
Burnup, Peter, 59

Casey, Pat, 144
Churchill, Winston, 21, 22, 88
Clancy, Basil, 174
Clark, John, 190
Coffey, Mr & Mrs Patrick, 64
Coffey, Patrick, 134
Collins, Michael, 22, 81, 91
Conboy, Martin, 117, 118
Connolly, Fr, 193-4
Conroy, C. M., 175
Conway, Mrs Patrick, 167
Cooper, Tom, 123
Cosgrave, W. T., 15, 21, 144-5
Costello, Joseph F., 131
Cox, Arthur, 183
Cresswell, Colonel R., 57

Crowe, Canon, 188
Cullerton, Mr, 130, 131, 132

Dalton, Emmet, 22, 90-2, 95-6, 179, 185
Dawes, Sutton, 182
de Valera, Éamon, 12, 13, 18, 20, 21, 22, 65, 68, 72, 81, 82, 84, 94-5, 98, 102, 117, 118-122, 170, 200-202
Delargy, Professor Seamus, 198, 200
Devane, Father, SJ, 127
Devane, R. S., 154
Devere, Frederick V., 189
Dillon, Dr Theo, 198
Dillon, James, 198
Ditcham, Frank, 160, 162
Dolan, Michael J., 122, 141, 145
Donovan, William J., 11, 12, 14, 50, 52, 53, 54, 65, 92-3, 109, 110, 111, 206, 207
Doyle, Dan, 134
Duffy, John, 187
Duquesne, Fritz Hubert (Major Craven), 30-2

Eckman, Sam, 158
Eisenhower, General Dwight, 89
Elliman, Louis, 141, 144
Elliman, Maurice, 143
Ellis, Gerald, 143, 175
Ellis, Jack, 157

Farley, James, 93
Ferdinand, Fr, OFM, 188
Fitzgerald, Geraldine, 177

Flynn, Errol, 15
Friedman, Joseph, 159, 160, 162

Gallagher, Frank, 137, 138
Garling, William, 160
Giltinan, Donald J., 105
Ging, Leonard, 175
Gray, David, 15, 16, 18, 19, 20, 67, 68, 103, 112, 117, 202
Guinness, H. E., 183

Hanley, Fr Thomas, 191
Harding, Warren, G., 47
Harley, Francis, 182
Hayes, Dr Richard, 22, 69-70, 77, 105, 117, 121, 122, 124, 141, 145, 154, 157, 163, 167
Hays, Will H., 47, 48, 66, 68
Hickes, John, 166
Hines, Monsignor John, 130, 132
Hogg, Lindsay, 177
Hoover, Herbert, 11, 110
Hull, Cordell, 13

Jones, Charles, 126

Kastner, Lacy, 166
Kearney, John D., 145
Kennedy, Thomas, 187
Kissane, Dr Edward, 185
Kitchener, Lord, 31

Landreth, Helen, 186
Littlewood, Robert, 162

MacEntee, Sean, 127
Marlin, Ervin Ross, 16, 17, 18, 19, 20
Martin, Joseph, 156
McCauley, Leo, 48, 157, 167, 177
McNally, Walter, 59-61, 61, 115, 116, 132
McPeake, B. Y., 154
McQuaid, Archbishop John Charles, 21, 23, 75, 199
Miller, Francis P., 47, 51, 52, 57, 76, 109, 110, 205

Milliken, Carl E., 53
Mountbatten, Lord Louis, 92
Mulcahy, Richard, 21, 179-80
Mulcahy, Timothy, SJ, 173
Mulligan, P. J., 189

Nicholas, R. Carter, 20, 54, 55, 64, 111, 112, 206
Norton, William, 127

Ó Briain, Liam, 131
O'Brien, Brian, 132
O'Brien, William, 187
O'Buachalla, Liam, 139
O'Curry, Peter, 134, 155, 168, 198
O'Farrell, J. T., 127
O'Higgins, Kevin, 156
O'Kelly, Sean T., 21, 105, 136, 137
O'Laoghaire, Liam, 176
O'Leary, J. J., 168
O'Malley, Ernie, 17
O'Meara, Harry, 14
O'Neill, Hugh, 85
O'Rahilly, Professor Alfred, 151
O'Sullivan, Martin, 142

Parsons, Wilfrid, SJ, 29, 50-1
Paton, Kenneth, 191
Patterson, Robert D., 13, 15
Power, J. A., 131

Quigley Publishing company, 31, 59

Ramsaye, Terry, 147
Rank, J. Arthur, 160, 161
Robbins, Frank, 150, 184
Robinson, Archbishop Pascal, 23, 70, 198
Roddy, Martin, 192
Roosevelt, Eleanor, 15, 21, 67
Roosevelt, Franklin D., 12, 14, 15, 68, 92, 93-4, 110
Rose, David, 166

Shanley, Fr Timothy, 185
Sheehy, Edward, 144
Sheehy, Terence, 177
Sheen, Monsignor Fulton J., 23, 121, 199
Shepardson, Whitney, 52, 53, 65, 110
Shipley, Ruth, 49
Silverstone, Murray, 182
Simon, Ernest, 166
Slocock, Mae, 73
Slocock, Viv, 73
Stanley, Joseph M., 81, 126, 142, 157, 175, 196
Stokes, Fr J. F., 196

Terrell, Dan, 127, 167-8
Tierney, Senator, 198
Toner, Edward, 176

Walker, Frank, 93, 117
Walsh, Roisin, 157
Walshe, Joseph P., 14, 15, 18, 20, 75, 102
Watts, Richard, 117
Wheelwright, Father Thomas, 23
Williams, J. D., 58
Wilson, Hugh R., 65
Wilson, Woodrow, 85

THE COURSE OF IRISH HISTORY

EDITED BY T. W. MOODY AND F. X. MARTIN

This is the best-selling history of Ireland ever published.
Originally published in 1967, it is still in demand all over
the world. The book provides a rapid short survey, with
a geographical introduction, of the entire course of
Ireland's history. It is designed to be both popular and
authoritative, with a wealth of illustrations.

MERCIER PRESS

HARRY BOLAND: A BIOGRAPHY

JIM MAHER

This is the first modern biography of a man who has been best known as a comrade and confidant – as well as rival in love – of Michael Collins.

As a member of the Irish Republican Brotherhood (IRB), Boland took part in the 1916 Rising and after his release from prison was appointed secretary to Sinn Féin. He played a prominent role in demanding political status for Irish prisoners in Britain. With Michael Collins he helped to build up the IRB and the Volunteers and organised the escape of Éamon de Valera from Lincoln Prison.

This volume gives a more comprehensive review of the six months prior to the Civl War (January to June 1922) than any previous publication. Boland's tragic death in the early days of the Civil War has gone down in popular history but this is the first time that the story of his last years and months has been fully told.

Jim Maher has spent many years researching the Civil War. He is also the author of a book on the War of Independence, *The Flying Columns – West Kilkenny.*

MERCIER PRESS

BROTHER AGAINST BROTHER

LIAM DEASY

Brother Against Brother is Liam Deasy's moving and sensitive account of the Civil War, Ireland's greatest tragedy. He recounts in detail the Republican disillusionment with the Truce and later with the Treaty, how the Republicans were hopelessly outnumbered, hunted and killed, especially in Munster, before they were finally broken and defeated. For the first time, Deasy recalls the circumstances surrounding his much-criticised order appealing to his comrades to call off the Civil War – an order that saved the lives of hundreds of prisoners.

Liam Deasy was born near Bandon in County Cork in 1896. He joined the Irish Volunteers in 1917 and on the formation of the West Cork Brigade of the IRA was appointed adjutant. He later became Brigade Commander. He took the Republican side in the Civil War and after it ended returned to civilian life, setting up a successful weatherproofing business. His celebrated account of the War of Independence, *Towards Ireland Free*, was published in 1973. He died in August 1974, while still working on *Brother Against Brother*.

MERCIER PRESS

WHEN THE NORMANS CAME TO IRELAND

MAURICE SHEEHY

When the Normans came to Ireland they established a political structure that was to last almost eight centuries. At no time during that long period did the political structure even loosely reflect the native identity.

The Ireland into which the Anglo-Norman crusade came in the twelfth century was culturally isolated from the rest of the world. The contemporary description of the Irish as an alien people represents not only the view from the nighbouring island but also the opinion of leading European administrators who come into contact with them. The crusade that we normally call the Norman invasion was a distinctly Christian venture. The motivation or justification for the crusade was only slightly more sophisticated than that which sent armies against the heathen during the same era. Maurice Sheehy deals expertly and lucidly with the conflict of cultural and religious identities at the time of the Norman invasion.

Maurice Sheehy, who was a lecturer in University College Dublin, was a classicist, philosopher and expert in medieval Church history. He died in 1991.

MERCIER PRESS

A SHORT HISTORY OF IRELAND

SEAN MCMAHON

This short history of Ireland has already established itself as a classic and a bestseller. A concise and even-handed account, it gives the history of Ireland since the earliest times. Based upon up-to-date research, the book covers all political, social and cultural issues of importance. The author is particularly enlightening about the root causes of the Northern Troubles and the relationship between Britain and Ireland.

MERCIER PRESS